A Short His
of the German L *g* *g*

A Short History
of the German Language

by

W. WALKER CHAMBERS

Professor of German,
University of Glasgow

and

JOHN R. WILKIE

Professor of German,
University of Aberdeen

METHUEN

LONDON **and** NEW YORK

First published 1970 by Methuen & Co. Ltd
11 New Fetter Lane, London EC4P 4EE
Reprinted four times
Reprinted 1984

Published in the USA by
Methuen & Co.
in association with Methuen, Inc.
733 Third Avenue, New York, NY 10017

© 1970 by W. Walker Chambers and John R. Wilkie

Printed in Great Britain by
J. W. Arrowsmith Ltd, Bristol

ISBN 0 416 18220 8

Contents

Preface

Students embarking on a study of the history of the German language often seem dismayed by the amount and range of unfamiliar detail which they are expected to control. They tend to lose their way in a field of study which should afford them both profit and pleasure. This short account of the subject may help them to obtain a knowledge of the main facts, chronological, geographical, and linguistic, and of how they fit together. We hope that simplification has not resulted in distortion and that the student will not only realize something of the scope of the subject but also acquire a reliable foundation for more advanced work.

Our aim has been to write a fairly orthodox account of the subject without entering much into the many controversies which dominate the field today. We have concentrated chiefly on the development of the standard literary language – the kind of German which British students know best and study most fully – and have reduced references to dialects and colloquial language to the essential minimum. We have also taken the risk of leaving aside all systematic treatment of phonetics and general linguistics (though Chapter 1 may serve as an appetizer). These subjects are of some importance even to beginners; but they are already treated in excellent introductory books, some of which are listed on page 7. Descriptive and structural linguistics lie outside the scope of this book – and may in any case be more appropriate for later stages of study.

The material is arranged in three parts. The first deals with the development of German from Indo-European onwards, against a background of the history (and prehistory) of the German-speaking community; the second covers the development of German vocabulary. These, it is hoped, are readable accounts which will give the student an impression of the development in its broad outlines. The third part surveys changes in sounds, forms, and syntax. These topics have been left to the end because they are the most arduous. It seemed more helpful to set out changes in sounds and forms in some detail, with examples, rather than to treat them in broad general terms. Because of this the final chapters can hardly be readable in

Preface

the ordinary way; but they constitute an important aspect of the subject and will, it is hoped, be more meaningful and therefore more manageable because of the perspectives offered in earlier chapters. Cross-references throughout the book indicate some of the many links between chapters.

The list of books for further reading at the end of each chapter has been restricted to a few specially useful titles; a fuller bibliography is to be found among the appendices. These also contain a table showing the development of strong verb classes and some representative specimens of medieval and modern German (with specimens of other Germanic languages for comparison); these passages may help to make the history of the German language more vivid and less abstract.

We gratefully acknowledge the valuable comments and other help received from colleagues and friends, especially from Dr Gillian Rodger and Dr W. R. W. Gardner in Glasgow, and from Dr C. D. M. Cossar, Mrs Susan G. V. Ellis, Mr J. E. Tailby, and Mrs Sheila R. Wilkie in Leeds; as well as from Mrs Pamela Freeman and Mr John Roberts, who helped with the maps.

In the 1978 reprint we have confined ourselves to correcting misprints and minor errors and must leave a more thorough revision to a later date. We are grateful to reviewers and others for helpful criticism and suggestions for improvement.

Glasgow and Aberdeen   W. W. C.
    March 1978   J. R. W.

Abbreviations

Only grammatical and linguistic terms are included here; other abbreviations should be intelligible from the context.

acc.	accusative	masc.	masculine
Alem.	Alemannic	MG.	Middle German
Bav.	Bavarian	MHG.	Middle High German
		mod.	modern
dat.	dative	neut.	neuter
EFranc.	East Franconian	NHG.	New High German
Eng.	English	nom.	nominative
fem.	feminine	OE.	Old English
Fr.	French	OFris.	Old Frisian
Franc.	Franconian	OHG.	Old High German
gen.	genitive	ON.	Old Norse
Ger.	German	OS.	Old Saxon
Gk.	Greek	part.	participle
Gmc.	Germanic	pl., plur.	plural
Goth.	Gothic	pres.	present
HG.	High German	sg., sing.	singular
IE.	Indo-European	Skt.	Sanskrit
infin.	infinitive	UG.	Upper German
L., Lat.	Latin	VL.	Vulgar Latin

In the tables in Chapter 12, N, A, G, D, I are used for nominative, accusative, genitive, dative, and instrumental; and M, F, N are used for masculine, feminine, neuter.

* indicates a hypothetical or reconstructed form (see footnote on p. 11)
\> stands for 'develops into'
\< stands for 'develops from'

Part I

CHAPTER 1

Language and language study

Man has been described as 'the talking animal', and language is one of the most pervasive elements in human life. Whether thought is possible without language is a question best left to philosophers and psychologists; but it is clear that in general our thoughts and feelings are given a measure of objectivity and permanence by being expressed in words. Social life, too, from the simplest personal contacts to the complex activities of nations, is unthinkable without language as a means of communication; indeed society could not have begun to develop at all if men had not been able, by means of language, to share their thoughts, to influence their neighbours' behaviour, and to transmit the heritage of experience. We no longer believe, as our remote ancestors did, that language in itself has magic properties; but anyone who has been moved by a great poet or novelist or stirred by a skilful actor or orator or preacher will need no further proof that language is a powerful instrument for good or ill in human affairs. The student of language can hardly be in doubt about either the interest or the value of his subject; at every turn he is involved in all the variety and complexity of human life and history.

But how did language begin? It is a reasonable assumption that the origin of language is in some way associated with the emergence of *homo sapiens* as a separate species. But in what circumstances and why did primitive man first begin to speak? What were the first human 'words' like? What were the early steps by which human language developed? Such questions have been asked at least since the days of Plato and the writers of the stories of the Garden of Eden and the Tower of Babel in Genesis; since the eighteenth century (since, for example, Herder's essay of 1772, *Über den Ursprung der Sprache*) interest in them has been continuous. But neither comparative philology nor the observation of the language of early childhood, neither the analysis of the language of modern primitive

3

societies nor the study of primitive man and the anthropoid apes has so far yielded more than a number of ingenious – but conflicting – theories. Such questions will no doubt continue to fascinate and tantalize us; but lack of evidence for a confident and convincing answer may well leave them for ever in the realm of pure speculation.[1]

In any case many linguists regard questions of the origin and early development of language as belonging to the fields of psychology, philosophy, and anthropology rather than to that of linguistics. They prefer to concentrate on those periods of language for which there is documentary evidence, either on modern languages and dialects, which can be observed directly and recorded on disc or tape, or on languages of earlier periods – languages now extinct or the older stages of extant languages – for which written documents have survived. This brings us to a much later date. For while man began to emerge between 250,000 and 500,000 years before the Christian era and *homo sapiens* was fully developed soon after 20,000 B.C., the earliest extant documents go back no farther than about 3000 B.C. These are texts in the Sumerian language (once spoken in the region between the Persian Gulf and Babylon), written on clay tablets in a cuneiform script (i.e. a script composed of wedge-shaped strokes). These are followed by texts in other languages as different communities reach a certain stage of civilization and invent or, more usually, borrow and adapt an alphabet. With this material linguists since the early nineteenth century have been able to construct an ever more complex picture of the world's languages and their development.

But they have also succeeded in penetrating into the pre-documentary period of language. By comparing the earliest extant forms of a large number of languages they have not only established relationships between languages which seem at first sight quite unrelated, but have reconstructed some of the features of undocumented languages from which the extant languages are descended. This has been done most successfully, as we shall see, for the so-called Indo-European group of languages, to which most European languages, including English and German, belong. But here two points must be stressed. In the first place, such reconstructions are only partial; the sound system is reasonably certain, grammatical forms and vocabulary are much more doubtful, while in the field

[1] For books on the origin of language see p. 8.

of syntax we seem unable to say anything very reliable at all. Despite the confidence of August Schleicher, who in 1868 published a fable in 'Indo-European', such a 'reconstructed' language is more akin to a skeleton than to a living organism. In the second place such reconstructions take us only a little way back – a few thousand years, perhaps – beyond the documents; they cast little light on the origins of human speech, which are separated from us by several hundred thousand years. At one time it was thought that it might be possible to compare the parent Indo-European language with the parent languages of other groups – Semitic, Polynesian, African, Chinese – and so to reconstruct the original human language, the *Ursprache*. It was widely believed that civilization and, with it, language, being such astonishing and unique phenomena, could only have arisen and developed from one place. But the other view seems at least as probable, namely that if language arose at one place it could just as easily have arisen at different places where conditions were roughly similar. At any rate the idea of a single original language is now much less widely held; and there seems little hope of penetrating to the origins of human language by such comparative philological methods.

But what *is* language, we may now ask, and how does it function? Language is a means of communication between minds and consists essentially of sounds (or groups of sounds) associated with ideas. This association seems to be quite arbitrary – apart from a small number of onomatopoeic words in which the linguistic sounds resemble the sound of the object or action named – but once it is established it is very close. When I wish to convey an idea to a listener, the idea in my mind at once evokes the group of sounds associated with it. These I articulate as physical sounds, which are received by the listener's ear. Finally the sound-group evokes the associated idea in his mind. This represents in a much over-simplified form the essential process of communication by language.

So far we have spoken of 'language' in a general sense. But a distinction must now be drawn between 'language' in a more restricted sense and 'speech'. Speech is a human activity, the individual act of speaking – or a series of such acts – a psycho-physical activity of the kind just described, without permanence but constantly renewed every time a person speaks. Language, on the other hand, is the whole elaborate system of 'sound-idea' associations. It is more than individual, being possessed by the whole community which speaks the language in question. Yet it is not an independent entity, for it

5

exists only in the minds of the individual members of the community. It is upon this store of established 'sound-idea' associations that the individual speaker draws in his act of speech, momentarily turning some small part of this passive, latent 'language' into active, concrete 'speech'. Language in this sense is a powerful social force. It binds a community together – for only through these established 'sound-idea' associations is communication possible on any large scale. By giving a certain permanence to the experiences and attitudes of the community it moulds the thinking and outlook of each new generation which learns it.

Language can be studied in two main ways, sometimes known as the synchronic or descriptive and the diachronic or historical methods.[1] The first aims at studying a language as it exists at a certain historical period, without concern for its development before or after that period. Such studies have shown that a language is not a mere jumble of 'sound-idea' associations, but a coherent system, an organic structure in which all the parts are complementary to each other. Yet it is not a fixed, immutable structure; on the contrary, it changes in small ways all the time. And any change in one part of the system brings changes in other parts. As some parts cease to function well – as, for example, ambiguity and obscurity creep in – other parts are adapted or created anew to do the work of the defective parts. In this respect a language is like a living body, where organs can adapt themselves to function in place of other diseased or missing organs. Most of these adjustments take place gradually and below the level of consciousness; only comparatively rarely do grammarians and linguists deliberately attempt to 'repair' and improve the language.

The aim of the historical method is to describe these changes in language and, if possible, to find their causes. The language may be studied in isolation, without reference to its human context; and this has been useful to establish the facts of change. It is more usual today, however, to study the history of a language along with the history of the community which speaks it, indeed in some sense as a record of that community's varying fortunes. For the causes of linguistic change seldom lie in the language itself, but rather in its human speakers. Linguistic changes, in fact, seem to begin with some individual who, for one reason or another, seeks to convey his meaning by a *new* association of sounds and ideas. If this innovation

[1] For introductions to the study of language see p. 7.

6

is imitated by other members of the community it ceases to be a mere personal idiosyncrasy and becomes itself an established part of the language. The reasons for any particular change, however, are not always clear. While it is often easy, for example, to account for the appearance of new words in the vocabulary, the reasons for apparently spontaneous changes in the sound system are often much more obscure.

So far we have treated languages in isolation. But in practice a language is related to a number – often a very large number – of other languages, and indeed in two ways. A number of languages may have developed from a common parent language; these are then said to be related genealogically. Or communities, living close together or separated by great distances, may have some connections, cultural, religious, political, social, or commercial, with each other. Their languages are said to be related culturally. We shall find examples of both these relationships in the history of German.

A short introductory book like the present one may give the impression that the history of the German language presents no further problems. In fact almost all the theories about the history of German which were once so confidently held have been questioned; over large areas of the field there is as yet no agreement. We shall be happy if some readers at least find in the following chapters a stimulus to investigate a few of the many problems which still await solution.

FOR FURTHER READING

Simeon Potter, *Modern linguistics*, 2nd edn., 1967
Mario A. Pei, *The story of language*, 2nd edn., 1966
Walter Porzig, *Das Wunder der Sprache: Probleme, Methoden und Ergeb-
    nisse der modernen Sprachwissenschaft*, 1950
Margaret Schlauch, *Language and the study of languages today*, 1967
Mario A. Pei and Frank Gaynor, *A dictionary of linguistics*, 1954

On phonetics:

David Abercrombie, *Elements of general phonetics*, 1967
Bertil F. H. Malmberg, *Phonetics*, 1963
Jethro Bithell, *German pronunciation and phonology*, 1952
Carl and Peter Martens, *Phonetik der deutschen Sprache: praktische
    Aussprachelehre*, 1961
Theodor Siebs, *Deutsche Hochsprache, Bühnenaussprache*, 18th edn., by
    Helmut de Boor and Paul Diels, 1961
Der große Duden: *Aussprachewörterbuch*, 1962

A short history of the German language

On the origins of language:

Arthur S. Diamond, *The history and origin of language*, 1959
Alexander Jóhannesson, *Origin of language: four essays*, 1949
Géza Révész, *The origins and prehistory of language*, 1956
Richard A. Wilson, *The miraculous birth of language*, 1937
Bernhard Rosenkranz, *Der Ursprung der Sprache: ein linguistisch-anthropologischer Versuch*, 1961

CHAPTER 2

Indo-European

The history of the German language begins, strictly speaking, with the appearance of the first written documents in the eighth century A.D. But German does not exist in isolation; it has close connections with other languages. In particular it shares with most European languages and some Asiatic ones a common origin in a language usually known among German scholars as Indo-Germanic and outside Germany as Indo-European. This ancient prehistoric language is, of course, entirely undocumented, but by comparing the oldest extant forms of its more important descendants nineteenth-century scholars were able to reconstruct some of its essential features.

Indo-European had a wide range of vowels,[1] ten monophthongs *a, e, i, o,* and *u,* both short and long, as well as a neutral vowel (sometimes called a 'schwa-vowel') noted as *ə* and pronounced like the unaccented final *e* in Ger. *Glaube*.[2] In addition six short diphthongs *ai, ei, oi, au, eu, ou,* were matched by six long ones *āi, ēi, ōi, āu, ēu, ōu.* The consonantal system was remarkably rich in plosives. In addition to the voiceless *p, t, k,* and the voiced *b, d, g,* there were aspirated forms of these, *ph, th, kh, bh, dh, gh,* as well as four labio-velars *kʷ, gʷ, khʷ, ghʷ,* in which the plosive element was combined with a *w* element and pronounced with rounded lips. Fricatives, on the contrary, were rare; only *s* and *z* are certain, though *þ* and *ð* (the voiceless and voiced 'th' sounds of English) may also have existed. The liquids and nasals *l, r, m, n, ŋ,* existed as ordinary consonants but could also function syllabically, i.e. in place of a vowel as the 'core' of a syllable (cf. the second syllable of Eng. *table*). This syllabic value is noted *l̥, r̥,* etc. Finally there were the semi-vowels *j* and *w.*

[1] Phonetic terms are explained in the surveys mentioned on p. 7.
[2] There is disagreement about the presence of other neutral vowels.

9

The accent was free and fell – in accordance with certain rules – on any syllable of the word; it also seems to have been predominantly dynamic (the accented syllable being pronounced more strongly or intensely than the adjacent syllables) and predominantly musical (the accented syllable being pronounced higher on the musical scale) at different stages of its development. There were two types of accent, an acute (with a single peak of intensity or pitch in the accented syllable) and a circumflex (probably with two such peaks).[1]

Declensions and conjugations showed a rich variety of inflexional forms. There were at least eight types of declension and a wide range of strong verb patterns. (Weak verbs did not exist in Indo-European.) The noun had three numbers (singular, dual, and plural) and eight cases (nominative, vocative, accusative, genitive, dative, ablative, locative, and instrumental). There were three genders (masculine, feminine, and neuter), which were grammatical as in modern German, not natural as in modern English. The verb had three numbers like the noun, four moods (indicative, imperative, subjunctive, and optative) and three voices (active, passive, and middle), as well as six simple tenses made without auxiliary verbs (present, imperfect, aorist, perfect, pluperfect, and future) and a number of infinitives and participles.[2]

A highly complicated inflexional system like this points to a long period of development. An Indo-European word is composed of several elements, one conveying the basic meaning and others indicating number, case, person, tense, mood, and so on. It is now widely assumed that at a very primitive stage of development each of these elements was an independent, meaningful word and that these words later coalesced to form inflected words. This process would be spread over a long period of time which it is impossible even to estimate.

But when was this language spoken? And, since a language implies a community of speakers, who were the 'Indo-Europeans', what was their civilization like and where did they live? The answers once confidently given by older scholars have been seriously questioned and there is much disagreement in the whole field. We no longer, for example, think of Indo-European as a fixed, static, unified language. Like all languages – at least until writing gives them a measure of

[1] *Acute* and *circumflex* as used here are to be distinguished from the acute and circumflex accents of written French.
[2] This grammatical system is best preserved in classical Greek.

stability – Indo-European must have been constantly changing and the features summarized above may have emerged at widely different periods of development. Again, Indo-European is unlikely to have shown complete uniformity over an extensive geographical area; even if its speakers were settled in a comparatively restricted area, it is more likely to have consisted of a group of dialects, each shading into the next (as modern dialects do) and all sharing some common features of sounds, grammar, and vocabulary.

One feature pointing to dialectal differences was noticed early. In some eastern descendants of Indo-European, notably the Indian, Persian, Armenian, Albanian, Slavonic, and Baltic groups, the front *k* sound developed into an *s* or *sh* sound, while in the Greek, Latin, Celtic, and Germanic groups it remained a plosive *k*. For example, IE.* *ǩmtóm*[1] 'hundred' is represented in Old Indian *śatám* and Old Persian *satəm* but in Latin *centum* and Greek *he-katón*. (The initial sounds of Eng. *hundred* and Ger. *hundert* also represent *k*, but have been changed by later developments.) This distinction between *satem* and *centum* languages – the Persian and Latin words are used as convenient labels – may well represent a distinction within Indo-European, but it is only one of many such distinctions, some of which cut clean across the '*satem–centum*' boundary. Indeed, it is possible that the new sounds developed in the language groups concerned after they had separated from the parent community. The '*satem–centum*' distinction must not be isolated and overstressed.

As regards date, the earliest documented groups of languages, Indian, Hittite, and Greek, had developed their separate characteristics soon after the middle of the second millenium B.C. and must already have undergone a long separate development. This would seem to support the older view that the Indo-European community and its language were still intact about the middle of the third millenium (very roughly about 2500 B.C.) towards the end of the Neolithic period, though it is possible that the break-up had begun much earlier.

The questions of the civilization and home of the 'Indo-Europeans'[2] is closely bound up with the Indo-European vocabulary. Vocabulary

[1] The asterisk is used to mark hypothetical forms, which are not recorded in any known text but have been reconstructed by comparative methods (cf. Chapter 1, pp. 4, 5).
[2] We know nothing about the racial composition of 'Indo-European' society. The name indicates a *linguistic* community and nothing more. Nor is it possible to say that the speakers of modern Indo-European languages are the descendants of the ancient speakers of Indo-European.

is a notoriously unstable aspect of language. Old words disappear, new words are coined or pass freely from language to language, and the meaning of words is constantly changing. The presence of a word in even a large number of Indo-European languages is therefore no guarantee of its existence in the parent language; nor is the meaning of the word in the parent language assured by its meaning (or meanings) in the extant languages. Nevertheless enough is probably known about the vocabulary to say that the Indo-Europeans had reached a comparatively high level of civilization. They were both warriors and farmers, cultivating a variety of crops and rearing various domestic animals. They were nomads, but built permanent houses, and they used simple tools such as ploughs, carts, and boats. They knew one metal, probably copper. The family was an important social and legal institution, and in their community some were free and some were not. They had developed the legal concepts of marriage, blood revenge, and wergeld. They worshipped gods, probably among others a god of light. And they had names for such natural features, flora, and fauna as were important in their life.

Vocabulary has been used to try to identify the region where the Indo-Europeans lived. Some scholars have studied the trees known to the Indo-Europeans, in particular the word *beech* and its corresponding words in other languages, in the hope of delimiting some geographical area. Others have studied fish names, especially the word-family represented by Ger. *Lachs* 'salmon'. But the great difficulty of discovering exactly which trees and which fish are designated by these words in Indo-European has prevented any conclusive results from being reached. Still others have sought to clarify Indo-European connections with the sea, only to be forced to admit that the evidence points either to the ocean or to a large inland sea. The most recent approach through place-names, and especially river names, has the advantage that the names are attached to definite localities and natural features and often survive through many changes of population and language. This approach seems hopeful but so far has not produced a definite answer.

An early theory claiming India as the probable home of the Indo-Europeans was linked with the mistaken belief that the ancient Indian language Sanskrit was itself the parent of the Indo-European languages or was at least the most closely akin to the parent language. This theory has long been abandoned. Two theories are now mostly

12

favoured. One, held mainly by some German scholars, looks to the north and north-east of Europe on the shores of the Baltic. The other favours an area north of the Black Sea and Caspian Sea. The latter may be preferable as pointing to a region more suitable for the development of a primitive civilization, though the linguistic evidence fits both tolerably well. Archaeology, which is now involved in the search, may in the end produce some significant material which can be associated with the Indo-Europeans and may thus point the way to a solution. Meanwhile the question remains unanswered.

In course of time the Indo-European community split up, for reasons which we do not know. They may have been driven by bad harvests to seek more productive land or tempted by prospects of conquest and wealth among less warlike people. We only know that at the dawn of history speakers of Indo-European languages were established over wide areas of Europe and Asia. We can distinguish ten major groups of languages and about half-a-dozen minor ones. The major groups are:

1. Indian, represented in its early stages by the two literary languages, Vedic, the language of the ancient Brahman hymns or Vedas, some of which go back to before 1000 B.C., and Sanskrit, the classical literary language of the Indian epics, dramas, and lyrics (fifth century B.C. to seventh century A.D.). The group also includes Prakrit and Pali, the latter being the literary language of South Indian Buddhism. The modern Indian vernaculars include Hindi, Urdu, Bengali, Marathi, Punjabi, Bihari, Sinhalese. Most modern gipsy languages are also of Indian origin.
2. Iranian, including Avestic, the language of the sacred writings of the Zoroastrians, and Old Persian, preserved in stone inscriptions from the time of Darius I and Xerxes on (i.e. from *c.* 520 B.C.), Middle Persian (notable in the early centuries of the Christian era), and New Persian (recorded from *c.* A.D. 900). Modern dialects include Afghan, Baluchi, Pamir, and Ossetic.
3. Armenian, first documented in a translation of the Bible from the fifth century A.D. Modern Armenian took shape in the fifteenth century. Nothing is known of the earlier history of this group.
4. Albanian, which may be connected with ancient Illyrian but is not its direct descendant. It is not recorded until the sixteenth

13

century. The problems of its relationships with other Indo-European languages are complicated by the presence in Albanian of many borrowings from other Indo-European groups.

5. Baltic, now represented by Lettish and Lithuanian. The latter is one of the most conservative of all Indo-European languages and has preserved many features of the parent language not found elsewhere. A third member of the group, Old Prussian, became extinct in the seventeenth century. (Old Prussian, it should be noted, was *not* a Germanic dialect.)

6. Slavonic, divided into South Slavonic (Bulgarian, Serbo-Croat, and the Slovene of Carinthia and Styria in Austria), East Slavonic (Russian in its various forms), and West Slavonic (Czech, Slovak, Polish, the Sorb of the Slav settlements in Saxony and Silesia). The oldest extant form of Slavonic is Old Bulgarian, also known as Old Church Slavonic, which had an influence throughout the Slavonic world as a liturgical language of the Orthodox Church.

7. Greek (Hellenic), whose earliest documents are the Homeric poems (eighth century B.C.), and which appeared in classical times in various dialects, principally Attic, Ionic, and Doric. In the post-classical period there developed a common literary and colloquial language, the so-called *Koinē*, which superseded the different dialects. In it the New Testament was written and from it modern Greek has developed.

8. Italic, represented chiefly by Latin, whose earliest texts date from the sixth century B.C. and which became the international language of medieval Europe. From Latin the Romance languages (Italian, Sardinian, Portuguese, Spanish, Catalan, French, Provençal, Rhaeto-Romanic, Rumanian) are descended. Before the ultimate triumph of Rome in Italy, Oscan and Umbrian were also important.

9. Celtic, including the ancient Gaulish language which was superseded by the Latin of the Roman conquerors. The Celts once occupied large areas in Central and Eastern Europe, extending as far as Asia Minor (cf. the Galatians of the New Testament). The modern Celtic languages fall into the Brythonic group (Welsh and Breton as well as Cornish, which has been extinct since the eighteenth century) and the Goidelic group (Irish and Scots Gaelic and Manx). They are mostly declining before the spread of English and French.

14

10. Germanic, which we shall examine in detail in Chapter 3. To it belong German and English, Dutch, Flemish, and Frisian, and the Scandinavian languages, as well as the now extinct Gothic.

A mere mention must suffice for the Tocharian of East Turkestan and the Hittite of Asia Minor, both long extinct but well documented, and a number of lesser groups, Lycian, Lydian, Phrygian, Pelasgian, Thracian, Illyrian, Venetic, etc., known only in proper names and scanty documents.

How are we to picture the disintegration of the Indo-European community and the development of separate languages? In the first place, the process was probably very slow, different groups breaking away at widely different times. Secondly, it did not happen in an otherwise uninhabited world. Indo-European itself was in contact with Babylonian and probably borrowed from it the ancestors of Ger. *Stern* and *Beil* as well as the rudiments of the duodecimal system of counting (still seen in the English tendency to reckon in dozens). The languages of the separated groups almost certainly adopted features of the non-Indo-European languages which they encountered and often superseded. Thirdly, life in new geographical and climatic environments produced new linguistic needs, which led to modifications of the inherited language. Finally, the separate groups did not lose contact with their fellow Indo-Europeans; their languages continued to influence each other through word-borrowings and the development of new common features away from the parent community. In short, the process is not a simple and tidy one of constant division and subdivision, as the family-tree type of diagram often used in this connection seems to suggest, but a very complex one, different for each language and probably impossible to reconstruct in any detail.

This kind of contact between groups can, however, sometimes be traced. Indian and Iranian have so many similarities that they are often referred to by the single name of Aryan[1] (from Skt. *arya* 'noble'). Baltic and Slavonic have many common features, though the idea of a common Balto-Slavonic language is now discredited. Germanic has features of vocabulary and grammar which it shares only with Italic, and others which are paralleled only in Baltic. Its

[1] This is the only correct use of the term. It should not be used to describe the whole Indo-European family – and it has no racial connotations. It must also be distinguished from *Arian*, which is connected with Arianism, a fourth-century Christian heresy!

early contacts with Celtic, however, are more superficial, being confined to Celtic words borrowed into Germanic.

FOR FURTHER READING

William B. Lockwood, *Indo-European Philology, Historical and Comparative*, 1969.
Otto Schrader, *Die Indogermanen*, 4th edn., by Hans Krahe, 1935
Thomas Hudson-Williams, *A short introduction to the study of comparative grammar (Indo-European)*, 1935
Hans Krahe, *Sprache und Vorzeit*, 1954
Walter Porzig, *Die Gliederung des indogermanischen Sprachgebiets*, 1954

CHAPTER 3

From Germanic to German

At some time during the disintegration of the Indo-European community a group of tribes made their way to north-west Europe, the area round the western end of the Baltic comprising South Sweden, Denmark, and Schleswig-Holstein. Here they developed a Bronze Age culture. This migration was probably nearing completion by *c.* 2000 B.C. In course of time the Indo-European dialect of the settlers underwent a number of far-reaching changes which made of it a new language, known as Germanic[1] or Primitive Germanic. We have no detailed evidence for the early movements of the Germanic tribes nor for the development of their language. A few Germanic words are indeed preserved in Latin writers such as Julius Caesar and Tacitus and in a few borrowings in Finnish and elsewhere. Otherwise Primitive Germanic, like Indo-European, is undocumented. Nevertheless with the help of archaeology and by comparing the oldest extant documents in Germanic languages we can reconstruct at least some features of this prehistoric period.

In their new homeland the migrating Indo-European tribes almost certainly found the territory already occupied by other inhabitants with different ways of life and a different form of language. As these original inhabitants learned the language of the invaders, some of their original speech habits – especially habits of pronunciation – will have been transferred to the new Indo-European and helped – though no doubt only as one cause among several – to produce the changes which distinguish Primitive Germanic from Indo-European. (Any visitor to Alsace or Lorraine will understand the effect of such a 'substratum' of old speech habits when he hears the French spoken

---

[1] It is important to distinguish between *Germanic* (Gmc.= *germanisch*) and *German* (Ger.= *deutsch*). There is no good English equivalent of *Germanen* to designate speakers of Germanic dialects. We shall use the Latin form *Germani* or such phrases as 'Germanic tribes', 'Germanic peoples'.

17

by German speakers and the German spoken by French speakers in that area.) These changes may be summarized as follows:

> (*a*) The First or Germanic Sound-Shift, affecting all plosive consonants;
> (*b*) A number of vowel changes;
> (*c*) The fixing of the accent on the root syllable of the word;
> (*d*) A great reduction of forms in declensions and conjugations;
> (*e*) The development of a second, 'weak' declension of adjectives;
> (*f*) The development of 'weak' verbs.[1]

We do not know how long such changes took to complete; not all of them were completed before the Germanic languages separated from each other. It is estimated that the First Sound-Shift was completed by *c*. 500 B.C.; but we only know that it was finished before the Germanic peoples established contact with the Romans in the first century B.C., since none of the words borrowed from Latin were affected by it.

Meanwhile the Germanic tribes had not remained static in their Scandinavian home. The region was not particularly hospitable, much of the coastal land was liable to flooding, and an expanding population needed more food and more land. Coupled with this went a sheer love of military conquest. Raiding expeditions by the young warriors of the tribe in spring and summer would give way to full-scale migration, groups from various tribes banding themselves together to seek a new home – preferably in good land conquered from less warlike neighbours, for this was much to be preferred to the labour of clearing trees and scrub from uncultivated tracts. This movement of expansion and migration had already begun before 1000 B.C.; it did not end until well into the Middle Ages. In this long period there can hardly have been a time when larger or smaller groups of tribesmen were not on the move; and at certain periods, particularly between the fourth and sixth century A.D. (the period of the so-called *Völkerwanderung* in the narrow sense) the whole Germanic world seems to have been in fairly constant turmoil, whole tribes and confederations of tribes moving very long distances at remarkable speed.

---

[1] For details of these changes see Chapters 10 and 12, as follows: (*a*) p. 99 ff., (*b*) p. 95 ff., (*c*) p. 102, (*d*) p. 119 and p. 128 f., (*e*) p. 126, (*f*) p. 129.

PRIMITIVE GERMANIC TRIBES

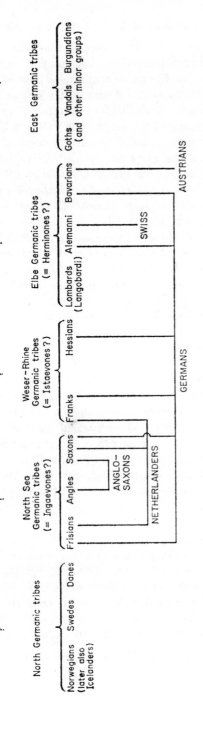

?	?	?	?	?
North Germanic tribes	North Sea Germanic tribes (= Ingaevones ?)	Weser-Rhine Germanic tribes (= Istaevones ?)	Elbe Germanic tribes (= Herminones ?)	East Germanic tribes
Norwegians (later also Icelanders) Swedes Danes	Frisians Angles Saxons	Franks Hessians	Lombards (Langobardi) Alemanni Bavarians	Goths Vandals Burgundians (and other minor groups)

ANGLO-SAXONS

NETHERLANDERS

GERMANS

SWISS

AUSTRIANS

Note: Very little is known about the steps which led from the original primitive Germanic community to the five tribal groups of the early Christian era. No attempt is made to represent these steps here.

Very early a few settlers had penetrated far into the north of the Scandinavian peninsula, but most migrants had turned southwards into the heart of the European continent. By the beginning of the Christian era the expansion had reached the Vistula in the east and the Rhine in the west, while farther inland the Main had long been passed and Germanic tribes were pressing southwards at the expense of Celts and Illyrians, when they were brought to a halt on the frontiers of the Roman Empire.[1]

For the period around the birth of Christ five great confederations of Germanic tribes may be discerned (on archaeological rather than linguistic evidence): the *North Germani* (later Swedes, Danes, and Norwegians) in Scandinavia; the *East Germani* (chiefly Goths, Vandals, and Burgundians) between the Oder and the Vistula, many of them very recently arrived from Scandinavia; and three groups probably corresponding to Tacitus's Ingaevones, Istaevones, and Herminones (*Germania*, 2, 3): the *North Sea Germani* ('Ingwäonen'; Frisians, Angles, and Saxons) on the North Sea coast; the *Weser-Rhine Germani* (chiefly Franks) between the Weser and the lower Rhine; and the *Elbe Germani* (including Alemanni, Bavarians, and Lombards) on the middle and lower Elbe.

We need not follow the fortunes of these various tribes in detail; but we must at least note that in course of time, mostly in the fourth, fifth, and sixth centuries, Goths and Vandals disappeared as separate peoples, Burgundians were established in south-east France, Lombards in northern Italy, Alemanni and Bavarians in southern Germany, Angles and some Saxons in Britain, and West Franks in northern Gaul. Lombards and West Franks gradually gave up their Germanic languages in favour of Romance ones. The Viking raids, the settlement of Iceland and the Norman conquest of Sicily and England were the last episodes in this movement of Germanic peoples.

The stabilizing force which emerged as the Germanic world at last came to rest was the Frankish Empire. Beginning with Clovis (king 481–511) and culminating in Charlemagne (king 768–814, crowned emperor of the West 800), the Franks, by conquest or peaceful annexation, gradually drew together under their dominion all the Germanic peoples of continental Europe. Only the Scandinavian north and Anglo-Saxon Britain remained separate, though contacts between England and the Frankish Empire were often close.

[1] For the groups of Germanic tribes and their relationships compare the diagram on p. 19.

From Germanic to German

It is against this shifting, unstable background that we must see the history (or rather pre-history) of the German language.

The first documents in the Germanic dialects appear at very different dates. Some Scandinavian runic inscriptions may go back to the later second century A.D., but for continuous Scandinavian texts we must wait until the eleventh century. The first continuous text in any Germanic language is the remarkable translation of the Bible into Gothic by Bishop Ulfilas (311–383). It is our only substantial record of the East Germanic dialects. In the west, English texts first appear in the late seventh and eighth centuries, and then in four dialects, West Saxon, Kentish, Mercian, and Northumbrian (the two last known together as Anglian). German texts begin *c.* 770 and become more numerous in the ninth century. They show a group of German[1] dialects of some complexity. In the north the Saxon dialect (known as Old Saxon, to distinguish it from the Saxon of England, and later as Low German or Low Saxon) stretched from the Zuyder Zee to the Elbe and farther east into Schleswig-Holstein, with its southern boundary in the Harz region. In a narrow coastal area running from the Zuyder Zee to Denmark and including the coastal islands were the Frisian dialects; but these are not recorded until the fourteenth century. West and south of Saxon lay a broad belt of Franconian dialects from the North Sea to the Upper Main. Low Franconian, the ancestor of Dutch and Flemish, lay south and west of the Zuyder Zee and covered roughly the area of modern southern Holland and Flanders. East and south of this were Middle Franconian, divided into Ripuarian (in the Cologne area) and Moselle Franconian (in the lower Moselle valley around Trier and Coblenz); Rhenish Franconian in the region of Mainz, Worms, Speyer, and Frankfurt and extending east to the river Werra; South Rhenish Franconian with its centre in Weissenburg (Wissembourg in Alsace); and East Franconian with centres in Würzburg and Bamberg. Between East Franconian and Saxon, and lying east of the Werra, was the Thuringian dialect, which is undocumented in the ninth century.

[1] We can now begin to use the term *German* (*deutsch*), though *deutsch* was in fact not used in this way until much later.

For the following discussion of German dialects see the map on p. 22. Dialect boundaries, unlike most political boundaries, are not sharply defined lines but more or less broad areas of transition between one dialect and the next. They sometimes change their position in the course of centuries. For the earliest period there is not enough evidence to trace boundaries at all. The map is, therefore, intended to show the main dialect *areas* rather than exact boundaries between them. For the sake of clarity only a few names of rivers are given to guide the reader. Other geographical features may be found on an ordinary map.

Finally, in the southern region of the Alps, Upper Rhine, and Upper Danube, and separated by the river Lech, lay Alemannic and Bavarian. Alemannic covered Swabia, Alsace, and large parts of Switzerland. In the most southerly part of this region, roughly modern German-speaking Switzerland, the dialect is known as High

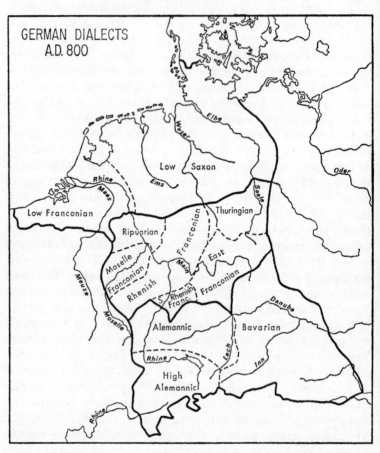

GERMAN DIALECTS
A.D. 800

Alemannic. Bavarian extended east to the region of Linz on the Danube. In broad outline, this is still the pattern of western German dialects today.

Some time before the ninth century some of these dialects had been affected by a series of changes in the Germanic plosive consonants which seems to have begun in the south – though scholars are not agreed whether the Bavarian or Alemannic or even the Lombard area of northern Italy is the place of origin – and to have had an ever decreasing effect on the dialects as it spread north and west. These changes are known as the Second or High German Sound-Shift,[1] and they provide a convenient means of classifying the German dialects. Saxon and Low Franconian, which are unaffected by the sound-shift, form the *Low German* group; the rest are *High German*. (Frisian is often omitted from this classification.) Within the High German group, Alemannic and Bavarian are most fully affected by the sound-shift and form the *Upper German* group, to which Lombardic seems also to have belonged. The *Middle German* group consists of East Franconian, Rhenish Franconian, South Rhenish Franconian, Middle Franconian, and Thuringian.[2]

The older way of accounting for the development of these Germanic dialects was to assume that Primitive Germanic divided into three branches: North Germanic, which later divided into an eastern branch (giving Swedish and Danish) and a western branch (giving Norwegian and Icelandic); East Germanic (represented by Gothic in which alone connected texts are preserved); and West Germanic, which divided into Anglo-Frisian, the parent of the English and Frisian dialects, and Primitive German, the parent of the High and Low German dialects. This 'family tree' is still useful as a classification of the Germanic dialects, but it cannot explain their growth. In particular there is no evidence that 'West Germanic' or 'Anglo-Frisian' or 'Primitive German' ever existed as unified dialects. It is true that 'West Germanic' languages share distinctive common features, just as there are distinctive features common to English and Frisian or to the German dialects. At the same time, within the German group Saxon in the north and Alemannic and Bavarian in the south are clearly opposed to each other at several points (quite apart from the influence or otherwise of the second sound-shift); and at these points Saxon is usually close to English and Frisian while Alemannic and Bavarian have parallels in Gothic or North Germanic or both![3]

An explanation of this state of affairs may well lie in the pre-history of the Germanic tribes. For the pre-Christian era we may

---

[1] For details of the Second Sound-Shift see p. 112.

[2] For the grouping of the Franconian dialects in later times see note 2 on p. 37.

[3] For example OHG. *andar*, Goth. *anþar*, ON. *annarr* (with a short initial vowel followed by a nasal consonant) contrast with OE. *ōðer* (Eng. *other*), OFris. *ōther*, OS. *āðar* (with a long vowel and no nasal consonant); cf. p. 96 f., point (9).

A short history of the German language

assume that dialectal differences were developing, but to what extent or how we cannot say. But the developments in the centuries following the birth of Christ may be at least partly explained by the five great tribal confederations which we noted above and within each of which, we may reasonably assume, there was a substantial measure of linguistic uniformity. The North Sea group (Frisians, Angles, Saxons) would account for similarities between English and Frisian and between these and Old Saxon. The parallels between Alemannic, Bavarian, Gothic, and North Germanic may be explained by the comparatively late dates at which Elbe Germani and Goths separated from their Scandinavian home as well as by contacts between Elbe Germani and Goths in the Oder region. Finally the common 'West Germanic' features may be due to closer relations between North Sea, Weser-Rhine, and Elbe Germani (=Ingaevones, Istaevones, Herminones?) in north-west Germany. The features common to all the German dialects, on the other hand, are probably secondary ones, which owe their dissemination to the political and cultural dominance of the Frankish Empire. If this theory is correct – and it is not universally accepted, for many obscurities still remain – German may now be seen, not as an original unity which broke into separate parts, but as a drawing together of separate dialects in the context of a common political and cultural life. A symbol of this late-found unity is the preposition *von/van*, shared by all the continental Germanic languages including Frisian, and unknown in Gothic, English, and the Scandinavian north.

FOR FURTHER READING

Antoine Meillet, *Caractères généraux des langues germaniques*, 7th edn., 1949
Ernst Schwarz, *Germanische Stammeskunde*, 1956
Friedrich Maurer, *Nordgermanen und Alemannen: Studien zur germanischen und frühdeutschen Sprachgeschichte, Stammes- und Volkskunde*, 3rd edn., 1952
Ernst Schwarz, *Goten, Nordgermanen, Angelsachsen: Studien zur Ausgliederung der germanischen Sprachen*, 1951

24

CHAPTER 4

Writing and printing

We have now reached the point where writing enters the history of the Germanic language. From the late eighth century until the invention of the phonograph in the nineteenth we are almost entirely dependent for our knowledge of German on written and printed records. In this chapter, therefore, we shall look briefly at the provenance of the German alphabet and its development in writing and printing till our own day. Readers who wish to omit this excursus should turn to Chapter 5.

As long as society is very simple and men's loyalties and interests hardly extend beyond their village or tribe, the spoken word is adequate for communication. Indeed such institutions as tribal assemblies provide sufficient means of communication even in fairly complex societies and scattered communities. Peoples without writing have accurate and capacious memories. But when it becomes necessary to keep administrative, commercial, or historical records and to communicate over very long distances some means has to be found to supplement the ephemeral spoken word.

The earliest writing, however, seems to have had a less mundane purpose; it was a vehicle of magic or primitive religion. Drawings, scratched or painted on cave walls or on pieces of bone, wood, and other suitable materials, were almost certainly thought to have magic power. This sort of picture writing may go back as far as 15,000 B.C. and is characteristic of most primitive cultures. But even when we come closer to writing in the more restricted sense we find that writing still consisted of symbols reserved for a few initiates, soothsayers or priests who alone could interpret or read the mysterious signs. In this connection it is significant that the word *rune* denoting the oldest Germanic alphabet comes from a root meaning 'secret' or 'mysterious' and is connected with Ger. *raunen*, which originally referred to the uttering of incantations, while Ger. *lesen* originally meant 'to choose' (as *auslesen* still does), the pagan soothsayers being the men who know how to choose and interpret the runes. The idea of a professional class whose duty is to interpret the sacred writings is, of course, present even in the higher religions, including Judaism, Christianity, and Islam.

The oldest kind of writing consisted of ideographs, i.e. the written symbol (often a simple picture) represented the thing or idea directly without reference to any words (sound-groups). Chinese writing is still of this kind. A great step forward was taken when the written symbol came to represent, not the thing, but the word for the thing. This development is first seen in Sumerian and in Ancient Egyptian writing about 3000 B.C. The next step was to make the symbol represent a single syllable and finally only the initial sound of the syllable. The first form of such a purely phonetic alphabet was evolved among the Semitic peoples, probably in the fifteenth century B.C., and from this important principle of one symbol (letter) to represent one sound the peoples of Europe and western Asia have never departed, though its practical application has often been wretchedly inadequate, as English spelling shows!

The Semitic alphabet in its northern form consisted of twenty-two signs for consonants and none for vowels. (Biblical Hebrew, for example, had no vowel signs until the seventh century A.D.) This alphabet passed to the Phoenicians and thence, probably in the tenth century B.C., to the Greeks, who adapted some of the signs to represent vowels and added others for sounds unknown in Semitic, such as *ph* ϕ, *ps* ψ, and *ks* ξ. This Greek alphabet is the parent of all alphabets in eastern and western Europe. It was adopted – and adapted to suit widely different languages – largely as a result of political and ecclesiastical forces, notably the Roman Empire and the Christian Church. There are no 'national' alphabets in Europe, but all are variant forms of the Greek alphabet, though it may not be easy at first glance to recognize their common origin.

From the Greeks the alphabet passed to the speakers of Italic dialects, including Latin, probably via the Etruscans (whose language was not Indo-European) and probably in the seventh century B.C. The Italic speakers modified it to suit the sounds of their own language, taking only twenty-one of the Etruscan letters, to which they later added two, *y* and *z*, direct from Greek in the first century B.C. One important development by Latin scribes – and indeed by Greek scribes as well – was the invention of a cursive ('running')

26

script, in which the shape of the letters was modified to enable them to be written rapidly in groups without raising the pen. Since Latin was the common language of the Roman Empire and the western church, the Latin alphabet was adopted, with minor adjustments, for writing the various vernacular languages of western Europe. It was used for German (Frankish) words as early as the sixth century (the so-called Malberg glosses, vernacular technical terms in the Latin text of Frankish laws).

But there had been a Germanic form of writing before that, the runic alphabet[1] or *fuþark* as it is called from its first six letters. Its origin is still uncertain, but it seems most likely that it was derived from a north Etruscan alphabet modified by other influences, Celtic or more probably Latin. Germanic tribes north of the Alps may have known the Etruscan alphabet before the beginning of the Christian era; but the earliest runic texts go back only to the later second century A.D. They appear on movable objects of metal, bone, and wood as well as on fixed stones of various kinds. This no doubt accounts for the characteristic straight-lined, angular shapes of the letters, which would make them easy to cut in these materials.[2] The *fuþark* appears in different forms, a common Germanic form with twenty-four letters, an Anglo-Frisian one with thirty-three letters and a later Scandinavian one with only sixteen letters. It was most fully exploited in Scandinavia, where it was used extensively until the late Middle Ages, often for quite long texts; even here, however, runic texts in manuscripts are rare. In England and Germany only a small number of runic inscriptions survive; the German runes date from before 800, while in England runes did not survive the Norman Conquest. Their association with pagan religion and magic was one reason which led to their being abandoned in favour of alphabets with more Christian associations.

The Goths in the Balkans, for example, had used the runic alphabet. But in the fourth century they were converted to Christianity and Ulfilas translated the Bible into Gothic for them.[3] As a bishop of the eastern Church he naturally based the alphabet which he invented on the Greek one, though he added a few Latin and a few runic letters to meet the needs of the Gothic language. This alphabet, which later found a limited use among the eastern Goths, is seen to

[1] Specimens of this and later alphabets and scripts mentioned in this chapter may be found in G.Eis, *Altdeutsche Handschriften*, 1949.
[2] Compare p. 74, note 3.
[3] See p. 21.

great advantage in a magnificent manuscript of Ulfilas' Bible, the Codex Argenteus, now in Uppsala.

In the west it was not Greek but Latin which was the dominant language. Latin was the language of the Church, into which all the western Germanic tribes were gradually incorporated; and since the Church had inherited the culture of ancient Rome, Latin was the language of education, scholarship, and literature. It had long been the language of civil government and law, the administrators were either clergy or men trained in the monastic schools, and Charlemagne – unlike his English contemporaries – followed a deliberate policy of Romanization. So when German came to be written down, the monks and clerics, who alone had the education to write, used the Latin alphabet with which they were familiar, adapting it where necessary in a somewhat rough and ready way to represent the non-Latin sounds.

By this time, however, the Latin alphabet was written in a number of different regional scripts. One of these, the insular script, had developed in Ireland and spread to England. It was brought to the continent by Irish and English missionaries in the seventh and eighth centuries, and some of its characteristic features may still be seen in German manuscripts of the ninth century. By the late eighth century, however, the insular script and other variants were being superseded in western Europe by the Carolingian minuscule script. This beautiful and eminently legible script, with simple rounded letters well spaced out on the page, was at least in part a product of Charlemagne's Romanizing policy; the small letters (minuscules), as well as the capitals (majuscules) which were added later, copied some of the best features of ancient Roman writing. From such centres as Tours, Fulda, and Trier the script quickly spread throughout the Carolingian Empire. In it are written practically all the German texts which have survived from the ninth and tenth centuries.

From the eleventh century onwards the style of writing changed. Letters became taller and more angular and were written closer together on the page, often in linked pairs or groups, until by the thirteenth century a new type of writing had developed. This Gothic script, as it is called, with its possibilities of rich and intricate ornamentation, was in harmony with the general artistic trends of the age as these are seen, for example, in the great Gothic cathedrals. The epic and lyric poetry of the courtly age of German literature is

28

almost all preserved in Gothic script, some of it in illuminated manuscripts of great magnificence, of which the larger *Heidelberger Liederhandschrift* (*c*. 1310) is a particularly splendid example. Gothic script in various forms, some elaborately decorated for the copying of books, others more simple and less formal for everyday use, remained predominant in Germany until the sixteenth century.

The technique of printing with movable types, which Johann Gutenberg invented in Mainz about 1450, represented almost as great a revolution in the history of language as the invention of writing itself. The earliest printers, however, adhered closely to scribal traditions, even to the retention of many abbreviations. In Germany they also retained the Gothic script, which, under the name of *Fraktur* (i.e. a script with 'broken' upright strokes) has remained the most common German type until the present century, in contrast to England and other western European countries, which very early adopted Roman types. In the nineteenth century men like Jakob Grimm, Hermann Paul, and Wilhelm Braune tried to introduce Roman type (*Antiqua*); but their success was limited to a few scholarly publications. Between the two world wars a more successful attempt was made to introduce Roman type; and since 1945 few books have been printed in Gothic type, while all the main newspapers have now adopted Roman type. Only the ligature *ß* (for *sz*) is normally retained from the old type.

Similar changes have occurred in handwriting. A cursive form of Gothic developed in the fifteenth and sixteenth century and remained, with minor variations, the normal German handwriting until recent times. This so-called *Deutsche Schrift* could be written with great vigour and beauty; but it could also deteriorate into illegibility even more quickly than Roman cursive scripts of western Europe, and it constituted a real barrier between German and non-German writers. Nevertheless, it was only after the First World War that attempts were made to abandon it. In 1941 a *Deutsche Normalschrift* (a form of Roman cursive) was introduced in schools, and today the traditional handwriting is read and written fluently only by some older Germans. No doubt it will disappear completely from use before long.

After this excursus we return to the Old High German period to continue our survey of the history of German.

A short history of the German language

FOR FURTHER READING

David Diringer, *The alphabet: a key to the history of mankind*, 3rd edn.,
  1968
Ralph W. V. Elliott, *Runes: an introduction*, 1959
Gerhard Eis, *Altdeutsche Handschriften*, 1949
Joachim Kirchner, *Germanistische Handschriftenpraxis: ein Lehrbuch für
  die Studierenden der deutschen Philologie*, 1950
Sigfrid H. Steinberg, *Five hundred years of printing*, 1955

30

CHAPTER 5

Medieval German and the development of the standard language

The history of a language is the history of continuous and gradual change, with no sudden breaks which might mark the clear beginning of a new period. Nevertheless, for practical purposes it has been customary to divide the twelve hundred years of the history of the German language into four periods: Old High German (*c*. 770–*c*. 1050), Middle High German (*c*. 1050–*c*. 1350), Early New High German (*c*. 1350–*c*. 1650), New High German (*c*. 1650–the present day). Despite all criticisms these divisions are still useful ones and we shall adhere to them in the following chapters.

What, then, was German like in the Old High German period? In outward form it was much simpler than its Indo-European or Primitive Germanic ancestors. Declensions and conjugations had both suffered a drastic reduction in inflexional forms; the lost forms had been or were being replaced by prepositional phrases, compound tenses (made with auxiliary verbs) and other syntactical devices. Such inflexional forms as still existed, however, were fairly clearly distinguished from each other by endings containing a full range of unaccented vowels. Consonants had been strongly influenced by the second sound-shift and vowels by various changes, including the development of modified vowels (umlaut), though most of these are left unnoted in the manuscripts. As to syntax and vocabulary, Old High German as it is recorded[1] is a language of monks and clerics.[2] We have virtually no record of the living speech of the common people, who were still largely barbarian, with neither the desire nor

[1] That is, leaving aside the large amount of oral vernacular poetry which we know existed but of which we have scarcely any direct evidence.
[2] For details see p. 22 f. and p. 112 f. (second sound-shift), p. 105 f. (vowels), p. 106 (umlaut), p. 119 ff. (declensions), p. 129 ff. (conjugations).

the skill to write down their language. Instead we have a number – a very small number indeed compared with the wealth of Latin surrounding them – of texts written by clerics for their own purposes. (Even the *Hildebrandslied*, the battered and venerable representative of the pagan tradition of heroic poetry, seems to have acquired Christian features.) The Church was involved in widespread evangelism among the half-pagan Germanic tribes as well as in efforts towards a better education of clergy and monks, who often understood Latin very imperfectly. The greater monasteries – Fulda, Weissenburg, the Reichenau, and St Gallen, to name only the most notable – were centres of these activities and, with few exceptions, the Old High German texts were written to serve these ends.[1] Almost all of them were either translated from or based on Latin texts, so that it is not always clear whether syntactical features are native to German or are imitations of Latin syntax. The vocabulary reflects a remarkable process of addition and adaptation as translators and others struggled to develop the resources of the traditional language in order to convey the subtleties of the Bible, the liturgy and theological thought.

But perhaps the most distinctive feature of this period is the absence of a standard language. In Germany today we find a large number of regional dialects (*Dialekte, Mundarten*), each with its distinguishing features. These dialects are the speech of the common people. Above them is another language (the 'German' we learn as foreigners), which is the standard language for the whole of Germany. This *hochdeutsche Schriftsprache* – we may call it the standard German literary language or simply 'standard German' – is primarily a written language in which books, newspapers, official documents, etc., are composed and which is read and understood by all educated people. Between the dialects and the literary language lies the colloquial language (*Umgangssprache*) of educated speakers, which tends towards the ideal of standard German but is strongly coloured, especially in pronunciation and vocabulary, by the local dialects in each region.[2] 'Old High German', however, like 'Old English' or 'Old French', does not denote any single unified language, but is

[1] Otfrid of Weissenburg gives another reason for writing his *Liber evangeliorum* (*c.* 870) in 'Frankish' (i.e. German). By using German to tell the gospel story, he hopes to give it the prestige long enjoyed by Latin and Greek.

[2] Standard German is also, with minor permitted modifications, the literary standard for Austria and German-speaking Switzerland. In Switzerland all classes of society tend to use the local dialect as their spoken language.

merely the collective name for a number of dialects. A standard language implies the existence of a substantial number of people who can read and write and who have political or social or commercial contacts with people in other dialect areas. But in the Carolingian and early Holy Roman Empires trade within the empire or with countries beyond it had been much reduced in comparison with the ancient Roman Empire; the people lived in local self-supporting agricultural communities under a developing feudal system, with few interests or contacts outside their village or, at the most, their county or duchy. There was indeed one class which fulfilled the conditions for a standard language, the clergy (among whom we may include most civil administrators). But they already had their standard language, Latin, the language of the Church and – as a heritage from ancient Rome – of administration and law, of literature and scholarship, and of the only formal education then available, that of the monastic and Church schools. Attempts have been made to show that Rhenish Franconian, which Charlemagne and his family probably spoke, was established as the 'language of the Carolingian court' and was on the way to acquiring wider currency. But though Rhenish Franconian may have acquired some temporary prestige as the emperor's own language, all evidence points to Latin as the only standard language in this period.[1]

Nor do the extant documents represent the speech of the common people. They were produced by monks and scholars and were written in a language based for the most part on the dialect of the region where the monastery was situated but affected by other factors, including the provenance of the monks, and standardized – at least in spelling and possibly in grammar as well – within each monastery (or occasionally within a small group of closely related monasteries). Some of these 'literary dialects' or 'scriptorium dialects', as we may call them, seem to have maintained a standard of spelling practically unchanged over several generations.

The literature of the Middle High German period (*c*. 1050–*c*. 1350) is very different from Old High German literature. Its outstanding

---

[1] Old High German words quoted without reference to a particular dialect are normally in their East Franconian form. This is a purely practical measure, due to the fact that East Franconian is closer to modern standard German in its consonantal system than other dialects are; it does not imply that East Franconian was in any way superior to other dialects. The situation is different from the Old English one. In England West Saxon does seem to have acquired, for political reasons, a currency beyond its own region.

feature is the magnificent flowering of chivalric and courtly poetry which we associate with Walther von der Vogelweide, Hartmann von Aue, Wolfram von Eschenbach, Gottfried von Strassburg, and the anonymous poet of the *Nibelungenlied* – to name only its very greatest representatives – and which is unsurpassed in medieval Europe. Beginning about 1170, it reached its climax in the years around 1200 and by 1230 had already entered into a long, gradual decline which lasted until well into the fourteenth century. At the end of the period the German mystics – Meister Eckhart, Johannes Tauler, Heinrich Seuse, and others – though lacking the sheer literary brilliance of the courtly poets, also made a notable contribution to European thought and spirituality. Both these movements left their mark on the German language, above all on the vocabulary. In its formal aspects, however, Middle High German is not very different from Old High German. The main changes were a more systematic noting of modified vowels and a reduction of most unaccented vowels to either a neutral *e* sound (like the *e* in *Glaube*) or to vanishing point. This loss of full vowels in final syllables led to the collapse of the old elaborate system of inflexions and, in due course, to the gradual emergence of modern patterns of declensions and conjugations.[1]

The greatest contrast with Old High German, however, is provided by the development of a literary language which was more widely used than any single dialect and which enjoyed a high cultural prestige. The earliest form of this language arose on the basis of the Middle Franconian dialect in the region of the middle Rhine, where an active literary life had developed in the years between *c.* 1150 and *c.* 1180. So far as we can judge from the linguistic ambiguities of the extant texts, this was the language in which such early epics as Lamprecht's *Alexander* (1140–50), *König Rother* (1150–60), and *Herzog Ernst* (*c.* 1180) were composed. Symptomatic of its wider currency is the fact that Eilhart von Oberge used it for his *Tristrant* (*c.* 1170) instead of his native Low German (Saxon), while it also had some influence on the Limburg (Low Franconian) dialect of Heinrich von Veldeke's poems, including the first version of his *Eneit* (*c.* 1170), which was later rewritten (by Heinrich himself?) in High (Middle) German for the Thuringian court.

Towards the end of the twelfth century courtly literature chiefly

[1] For details see p. 106 ff. (modified vowels), p. 108 f. (unaccented vowels), p. 121 f. (declensions), p. 131 ff. (conjugations).

flourished in southern Germany and Austria and here, on a basis of Upper German, particularly of northern Alemannic (Swabian) and nearby East Franconian, the literary language of the great courtly poets developed. What part the Hohenstaufen emperors played in its development is debatable. Though they were themselves Swabians – and two of them, Henry VI and Conrad IV, were Minnesingers – they are hardly likely to have made any personal contribution. What is certain, however, is that the Middle High German literary language was a product of the courtly culture which owes much of its brilliance and self-assurance to the political success of Frederick I Barbarossa (1152–90) and Henry VI (1190–7). By avoiding merely local forms and expressions and by choosing rhymes which survived transposition into other dialects, the courtly poets built up a language which came to be used in all German-speaking regions, including Low German areas (though not in the Netherlands). Yet it was not a standard language in the fullest sense. It was, in the first place, by no means so uniform as modern 'normalized' editions sometimes suggest but had at least some dialectal colouring, however slight, in the usage of most poets. Despite its admirable flexibility of syntax and subtlety of expression it did not develop the resources needed to deal with the interests and activities of the whole of society. It was certainly not used by the common people, who continued to speak their dialects. The language of Church and State, of learning and administration, continued to be Latin – though indeed German was beginning to be used (Eike von Repgow's *Sachsenspiegel*, a legal text, *c*. 1222, and his *Weltchronik*, *c*. 1225; the first imperial law drafted in German, 1235). The Middle High German literary language is confined to one social group, the lay aristocracy, as the language of their imaginative literature and presumably also – though evidence for this is scanty – as a model for the spoken language of the courts, especially in their contacts with courts in distant dialect areas. With the decline of courtly society the courtly language gave way once more to the dialects. It was not the direct forerunner of the modern standard language, which grew from very different roots, as we shall see. And yet, was it a mere episode with no lasting effects? When the Low German towns of Göttingen, Münden, and Northeim entered into an alliance in 1336, the text of the treaty was in High German. This and other similar evidence suggests that the courtly culture of the Hohenstaufen period had so established the prestige of High German that when the new standard language did develop it was likely to be High German rather than Low German in character.

By the middle of the fourteenth century, when the Early New High German period (*c.* 1350–*c.* 1650) begins, the German-speaking area which we described for the eighth century[1] had greatly increased in size. A colonizing movement which had begun under Charlemagne and reached its peak in the twelfth and thirteenth centuries had carried great numbers of knights and missionaries, peasants and merchants eastward to take possession of vast areas beyond the Elbe, the Saale, and the Bohemian Forest, from Austria in the south, through the middle regions of Bohemia and Moravia, Meissen, the Lausitz and Silesia to Brandenburg, Mecklenburg, Pomerania, and Prussia, and on to the Gulf of Finland. Meanwhile here as in the old regions farther west – as indeed in the whole of western Europe – trade was flourishing and towns were growing rapidly. While clergy and aristocracy continued to play their part, the tone of society was beginning to be set by urban patrician families, merchants, and skilled artisans. In this increasingly complex society it was no longer possible to leave territorial and municipal administration to clerics trained in Latin. A need was becoming felt for a type of German which would be adequate for the legal niceties of chanceries (government offices), for the widespread contacts of merchants, and the technicalities of industry, for a literature which would appeal to educated burghers and for the whole range of human activity.

In the Netherlands such a language was rapidly developing. There the Middle High German literary language had had no currency, but a standard language based on Low Franconian and used both for practical purposes and for literature had arisen in the later thirteenth century. By the sixteenth century, with the political separation of the Netherlands and the establishment of a Calvinistic type of Protestantism, this language, rather than High German, was established as the standard for the Netherlands. From it have developed modern Dutch and Flemish.

In north Germany the lively commercial and social life of the Hansa towns led by the middle of the fourteenth century to the emergence of another regional standard language, which was used in most north German chanceries. The Hansa settlements in Scandinavia, the Netherlands, England, and Russia, as well as

[1] See p. 21 f.

36

adopting the Lübeck legal code as a model in towns all along the Baltic coast, gave it a wider prestige outside Germany than any other type of German before or since. For a time it was the commercial language of the whole of northern Europe, as well as being the vehicle of a lively Low German literature. But the decline of the Hansa brought a decline of the language, and by the end of the fifteenth century it was already being replaced by High German, though it contributed some vocabulary to the High German standard language.[1]

In colonial eastern Germany developments of more permanent importance were taking place.[2] The colonists of these new lands had been drawn from almost every part of the old Germany. In the Meissen region, for example, one stream of settlers can be traced from the Upper Main through Würzburg and Bamberg to the south of Meissen, another from west central Germany via Erfurt to the vicinity of Meissen itself and a third from north Germany via Magdeburg to a belt north of Meissen. This mixture of population, which was repeated with local variations in the Lausitz and Silesia, Bohemia and Moravia, led to the development – first in the Meissen region itself, but later in the whole East Middle German area – of a mixed colonial dialect containing northern, central, and southern features. Characteristic of this colonial dialect were the vocalic features which chiefly distinguish New from Middle High German: the new diphthongs *ei, au, eu* from MHG. *ī, ū, iu (ü)*, already seen in Bavarian in the twelfth century; the new monophthongs *ie (ī), ū, ü* from MHG. *ie, uo, üe*, a feature of Middle German origin; and the lengthened vowels in open syllables, which had their origin in Low German.[3]

This development coincided with the rise to power of the Wettin dynasty, which from its centre in Meissen spread its rule westward to encompass Thuringia and thus to lay the foundations of the powerful state of Saxony.[4] It is owing in large measure to the political

---

[1] See p. 78, note 2.
[2] For the following see the map on p. 38. The continuous heavy lines which serve as both the northern and southern boundaries of the East Franconian and South Rhenish Franconian area in this map (in contrast to the earlier one) indicate that these dialects, which were classified as Middle German in the ninth century, acquired, from Middle High German times, characteristics which brought them closer to Upper German.
[3] For details see p. 109 ff.
[4] The eastern German state of Saxony (*Sachsen*) with its (Upper) Saxon dialect must be distinguished from the old province of Lower Saxony in northern Germany, whose language from the Middle High German period onwards is usually called Low German.

power of the Wettin state, with its great commercial centre of Leipzig and its influential cultural and educational centre of Erfurt, that the mixed colonial dialect, shorn of its most obviously dialectal features, became the basis of a commercial and colloquial language which was used throughout the East Middle German region and from which

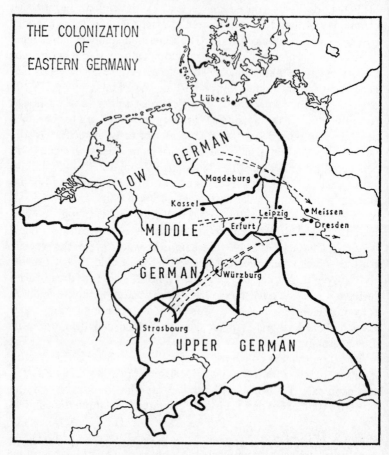

THE COLONIZATION
OF
EASTERN GERMANY

the various chancery languages of the region are derived. Two of these, the chancery language of Prague and that of Meissen (Saxony) itself, are of special importance.

The Prague chancery language came into prominence when Charles IV (1347–78) established the imperial court in that city. Under Charles's learned chancellor, Johann von Neumarkt, the chancery language became a carefully regulated instrument used not only for official documents but also for literary purposes in the remarkable movement of Bohemian humanism which represents the first impact of the Italian Renaissance on German literature and of which Johann von Neumarkt's own writings and Johann von Tepl's *Ackermann aus Böhmen* are the outstanding examples. But all this is no more than an isolated episode. The Prague chancery language was not, as was once thought, the model for other East Middle German chancery languages; the many common features which these share are derived from their common source, the mixed colonial language of East Middle Germany. With the removal of the imperial chancery to Austria (finally to Vienna) under the Habsburgs, the decline of Bohemian humanism, the Hussite wars and the establishment of a Czech national monarchy, Prague's linguistic influence was at an end.

The Saxon chancery language, on the other hand, had by the late fifteenth century gained considerable currency outside Saxony itself. Thuringia was an active centre of late medieval mysticism, while the Teutonic knights in Prussia had connections with Erfurt. The school of Erfurt had long produced scholars and administrators, not all of whom remained in Wettin lands. In northern Germany the Saxon chancery language was replacing Low German in several chanceries. In the west Albrecht of Meissen, on his election to the Archbishopric of Mainz in 1480, introduced many Saxon features into the Mainz chancery language; and since this was the language used for printing the *Reichstagsabschiede* (ordinances of the Imperial Diet) Saxon features were made familiar to chanceries throughout the Empire.

The last of the regional standard languages developed in the south. With the establishment of the imperial chancery in Austria (1438) and finally in Vienna the old chancery language inherited from Prague acquired Austro-Bavarian features. Through the efforts of Maximilian I (1493–1519) and his chancellor Niclas Ziegler this language was used for all imperial documents, whether written in Vienna or Innsbruck, Ghent or Brussels. It also became the model for a southern standard language, often referred to as *Das Gemeine Deutsch* (Common German) which was widely used in Austria and Bavaria, in Swabia, Alsace, and Basle (but not elsewhere in Switzerland) and in parts of the Rhineland. It was also used, with local variations, by the south German printers.

39

Printing was, in the long run, a unifying force in the development of German. The ability to produce large quantities of books at moderate prices and the desire to distribute them as widely as possible made the need for a standard language even clearer than before. But in the late fifteenth century there was no such standard and the printers used what was available, usually the local chancery language. We can distinguish some half-a-dozen printers' languages in the High German area and three or four in Low Germany, those in the south, used in the leading centres of printing such as Augsburg or Nuremberg, being variants of *Das Gemeine Deutsch*. Indeed in 1500 it must have seemed as if this language, already widely used in the south and backed by the prestige of the imperial chancery and the south German printers, was likely to become the standard for the whole of Germany. What in fact happened was quite different: the advent of Luther and the final victory of East Middle German (Upper Saxon) as the basis for the modern standard language.

Martin Luther (1483–1546) was a theologian and reformer, anxious to bring the Word of God to his fellow Germans and to restore the Church to its ancient purity. Language for him was simply a tool to help him achieve his purpose. As it happened, an effective form of German lay ready to hand in the language of his territorial chancery. 'Ich habe keine gewisse, sonderliche, eigene Sprache im Deutschen,' he is reported as saying,

> sondern brauche der gemeinen deutschen Sprache, daß mich beide, Ober- und Niederländer verstehen mögen. Ich rede nach der sächsischen Canzeley, welcher nachfolgen alle Fürsten und Könige in Deutschland; alle Reichsstädte, Fürsten-Höfe schreiben nach der sächsischen und unsers Fürsten Canzeley, darum ists auch die gemeinste deutsche Sprache. Kaiser Maximilian und Kurfürst Friedrich, Herzog zu Sachsen etc. haben im römischen Reiche die deutschen Sprachen also in eine gewisse Sprache gezogen.[1]

---

[1] Martin Luther's *Werke, Tischreden*, vol. 1, Weimar 1912, pp. 524–5: 'I have no definite, special language of my own in German, but use the common German language so that people from both the upper and lower territories may understand me. I speak according to the Saxon chancery, which all princes and kings in Germany follow; all the Imperial Cities and princely courts write according to the chancery of Saxony and of our prince, and for that reason it is the commonest German language. The Emperor Maximilian and Elector Frederick, Duke of Saxony, etc., have thus combined the German languages of the [Holy] Roman Empire into one definite language.'

In fact, of course, no such uniformity existed. Though the Saxon chancery language had been influenced by the southern *Gemeines Deutsch*, the differences were still many and obvious. Nevertheless, the currency which, as we have seen, the Saxon chancery language had acquired outside Saxony may well have made it 'the commonest German language'; what is certainly true is that Luther followed it closely as a model. But only in respect of outward, formal aspects. The stiff, involved, unemotional style and limited vocabulary of the chancery lawyers were clearly inadequate for the wide range of Luther's writings in German; in matters of vocabulary, idiom, and style he drew on other sources. The mystics and other religious writers of the late Middle Ages, whose works Luther knew intimately, had already gone far in adapting German to express theological and spiritual ideas. Besides, no fewer than fourteen High German and four Low German translations of the Bible had appeared between 1467 and the appearance of Luther's New Testament in 1522; these, on the whole, Luther found unsatisfactory in that they were too closely bound to the Latin text (see quotation below), but he was able to draw upon them here and there. But above all this man of peasant stock knew how to make effective use of the language of the common people. 'Man mus nicht die buchstaben inn der lateinischen sprachen fragen, wie man sol Deutsch reden,' he wrote in his *Sendbrief vom Dolmetschen* (1530) with reference to his Bible translation, '. . . sondern man mus die mutter jhm hause, die kinder auff der gassen, den gemeinen man auff dem markt drumb fragen, und den selbigen auff das maul sehen, wie sie reden, und danach dolmetzschen, so verstehen sie es den und mercken, das man Deutsch mit jn redet.'[1]

In what sense, then, may Luther be regarded as 'the father of the German language'? He invented no new standard form of the language, nor did he lay down rules for correct usage in spelling and grammar, as was once thought. In these matters he followed the Saxon chancery and was even somewhat old-fashioned and inconsistent, preferring older forms like *in* and *im*, *kreffte*, *geste*, or *ander*, and only adopting the more modern *yhn*, *yhm*, *kräffte*, *gäste*, and

---

[1] D. Martin Luther's *Werke*, vol. 30(ii), Weimar 1909, p. 637: 'We must not ask the letters of the Latin language how we are to speak German . . . but we must ask the mother in her home, the children in the street, the ordinary man in the market-place and watch their lips and see how they speak and translate accordingly; then they will understand it and notice that we are speaking German to them.'

41

zweit when they were already well established; and it was only comparatively late in life that he began to supervise personally the details of proof-reading and printing of his works. It is rather in his artistic handling of German that he was a true creator. Among his many gifts he had a remarkable feeling for the manifold variety of language and for its emotional nuances; and the richness of vocabulary, the felicity of idiom, and the vigour and directness of style which characterize all his works – Bible and hymns, catechism and sermons, expository and polemical tracts – mark a new beginning in the development of the German language. In particular, his masterly translation of the Bible, which in the four intervening centuries has been read and studied and learnt by heart more than any other German book, has had a profound and incalculable stylistic influence – to say nothing of its spiritual effect – on every generation of speakers and writers until our own day.

With Luther the decisive step towards the establishment of the New High German standard language had been taken. His own prestige and the rapid spread of the Reformation carried his writings, and especially his Bible translation, all over the German-speaking world, even to those regions which remained Catholic. The Saxon chancery language, as modified and developed by Luther, began its progress to final acceptance as the standard German language. There is much truth in Jakob Grimm's description of standard German as 'the Protestant dialect'. And it is significant that when Johannes Clajus published his *Grammatica Germaniae Linguae* in 1578 he used Luther as his norm – though it is equally noteworthy that from the second edition onwards 'Luther' is replaced by 'all the best authors'!

Yet this process was neither speedy nor simple. For one thing the language itself changed considerably in the centuries after Luther, chiefly in vocabulary, in its range and in the meaning of words, but also to some extent in grammar; and it adopted many features from other regions, especially from the south and the Low German region. In inflexional forms, however, and above all in sounds, standard German has remained on the whole East Middle German in character.

In the second place, while the confessional situation – the division between Catholic and Protestant and, among the Protestants, between Lutheran and Reformed – was important, other influences have to be reckoned with. Chanceries, printers, schools – which were often an outcome of the Reformation – humanism and the

42

general cultural situation played their parts, which were often conflicting and were different in the various regions of the country. We
can do no more here than give the briefest description of this long
and complicated development.

The Saxon standard was accepted most readily in Middle Germany. In the East Middle German region, as we have seen, it was
closely akin to the people's dialect, though even in this region protests
came from Martin Opitz and other Silesian writers in the seventeenth
century. In West Middle Germany, where the Saxon chancery had
had some influence before Luther's time, it was firmly established
wherever the Reformation took root. A symptom of this is the
establishment of Frankfurt, alongside Wittenberg, as the chief centre
for the printing of Luther's Bible. (Yet even in Goethe's early years
the language of Frankfurt had certain affinities to the southern
language.)

The north moved more slowly. Several chanceries had already
accepted the Saxon language; and the Reformation spread rapidly
throughout the area. But Luther's language was remote from the
people's Low German, and the language of preaching remained Low
German until after 1600. Luther's Bible was translated into Low
German – the New Testament as early as 1522 – and continued to
be printed until 1621. But by the early seventeenth century, most
official documents and literary works were written in High German,
though in some places Low German remained the colloquial language
of even educated people until the eighteenth century (e.g. in Bremen)
or even well into the nineteenth, as in Stettin.

The strongest opposition to the Saxon standard came in the south
and continued far beyond our period. In Switzerland political
opposition to the Habsburg regime was allied to the hostility of
Reformed Protestants to the Lutherans. Concessions came first from
the printers. In Basle they had accepted the new diphthongs *ei, au,
eu* (from MHG. *ī, ū, iu*) even before 1500; when they were accepted
in Zürich about 1630 it was to further a wider distribution of
Zwingli's Bible translation in opposition to Luther's. It was well into
the seventeenth century before the new diphthongs appeared in
public documents – after 1650 in the Zürich Council minutes – while
few concessions in vocabulary and idiom were made until much
later still. Even today the colloquial language of all classes is the
local dialect.

In southern Germany the confessional opposition to the Saxon standard was strong and the Counter-Reformation and the Jesuits only intensified it. It seems incredible to us today – as it finally appeared ridiculous to the south Germans themselves – that Luther's retention of final unaccented -*e* (*Glaube*, *Wölfe*), which was normally dropped in the south, was attacked with nearly as much ferocity as his Protestant doctrines. But the importance of this confessional opposition must not be exaggerated. Luther's remarks near the beginning of his *Sendbrief vom Dolmetschen* show how well aware he was of the influence which his Bible translation had in Catholic circles. The Catholic Bible translations of Hieronymus Emser (1534) and Johann Eck (1537) – the latter an Upper German version – are strongly influenced by Luther's translation. On the other hand, Hans Sachs of Nuremberg, a convinced Protestant, wrote in a version of the southern *Gemeines Deutsch*, while the Swabian Hieronymus Wolf, though a Lutheran who had studied in Wittenberg, defended the language of the imperial court as a norm. The real reason for opposition was cultural. The south already had a well established literary language and a rich literary tradition. What it did not see or was reluctant to admit was that the literary centre of Germany was moving northwards, to Leipzig and Dresden and, in the seventeenth century, to Silesia, while the south was turning to architecture and sculpture, painting and music, to produce in due course the magnificent – but not literary – monuments of south German Baroque. It was not until the middle of the eighteenth century that this opposition was overcome.

FOR FURTHER READING

Hugo Moser, 'Deutsche Sprachgeschichte der älteren Zeit', in Wolfgang Stammler (ed.), *Deutsche Philologie im Aufriß*, 2nd edn., Vol. 1 (1957), cols. 621–854

Arno Schirokauer, 'Frühneuhochdeutsch', in *Deutsche Philologie im Aufriß*, 2nd edn., Vol. 1, cols. 855–930

Hans Eggers, *Deutsche Sprachgeschichte*: Vol. 1 *Das Althochdeutsche*, 1963; Vol. 2 *Das Mittelhochdeutsche*, 1965

Kenneth Brooke, *An introduction to Early New High German*, 1955

CHAPTER 6

New High German

The German-speaking area has undergone many boundary changes since Charlemagne's day. But compared with the enormous expansion in the Middle Ages,[1] the last three or four centuries have seen much smaller territorial gains, as well as considerable losses, notably after the defeat of the National Socialist regime in 1945. In the west the Netherlands have gone their separate way since the late Middle Ages,[2] while the incorporation of Alsace and Lorraine into France in the seventeenth century led to increasing use of French by educated speakers, a tendency which was only temporarily halted between the Franco-Prussian War of 1870-1 and the end of the First World War in 1918 and again between 1940 and 1945, when Alsace and Lorraine were annexed to Germany. Even today, however, the local German dialects remain vigorous in country districts. In the south various north Italian communities which had once been German-speaking had virtually given up German before 1914; in South Tirol, on the other hand, the vigorous attempts made to suppress German after the province was incorporated into Italy in 1919 have been largely unsuccessful. In the north-east the 'Baltic Germans' were repatriated from Estonia and Latvia in 1940-1, while German has virtually ceased to be spoken in Lithuania since 1945. Polish and Russian have replaced German in East Prussia. In the east, Bohemia was largely lost in the fifteenth century, though Prague and the Sudeten German communities remained culturally important until 1945. As early as the twelfth and thirteenth centuries German settlements separated from the main German-speaking area had been established in Rumania (Siebenbürgen) and Slovakia (Zips), and these were followed in the eighteenth century by extensive settlements in Hungary, South Russia, and Poland. Only a few of these settlements – the largest is still Siebenbürgen – have survived after 1945. In the territories east of

[1] See p. 36.   [2] See p. 36.

the rivers Oder and Neisse, which were annexed to Poland in 1945, German has become the language of a small minority and the dialects of that region are approaching extinction. In large areas of central and eastern Europe Yiddish (from Ger. *jüdisch* 'Jewish'), a language basically German but with many Hebrew elements, has been extensively used by Jewish people since the Middle Ages. Outside Europe German was widely used in Africa until the loss of Germany's African colonies in 1918. German speakers have also emigrated to North America since the seventeenth century and to South America since the nineteenth, often to escape from religious or political oppression at home. The communities they founded still flourish in some places, notably in Pennsylvania, and still use a form of German, in which newspapers and books are printed.

More important to us, however, than the distribution of German speakers throughout the world are the linguistic developments in the main German-speaking area during the New High German period (*c.* 1650 to the present day). The first part of the period was dominated by two questions. In the first place, which type of German was finally to become the standard language? Would the south finally accept the Upper Saxon (East Middle German) type, as the north and east (and to some extent the west) had already done? But secondly – and more seriously – was German in any form really fit to fulfil the manifold needs of society, as a written language for literature and scholarship of all kinds and as a spoken language in polite society?

In the seventeenth century Latin was still the language of scholarship and serious literature. The heritage of ancient Rome and the prestige of the monastic and cathedral schools and later of the universities had given it a firm place throughout western Europe. In Germany, the humanism of the fifteenth and sixteenth centuries only confirmed its predominance. In contrast to the rest of western Europe, which saw a remarkable flourishing of vernacular literature at this time, most of Germany's finest literary verse and prose was in Latin, while writings in the vernacular were dominated by the themes and problems of the Reformation and Counter-Reformation. Even Luther, the reputed father of the German language, wrote more Latin than German. In 1570 seventy per cent of all books printed in Germany were in Latin, and even at the beginning of the eighteenth century the proportion was still some thirty per cent. The last strongholds of Latin were the universities. Paracelsus had lectured

46

in German at Basle in 1526–7, but his example was not followed until
1687, when Christian Thomasius began to lecture in German at
Leipzig. German was recognized as the teaching language at Halle
in 1700 and at Göttingen in 1733. The power of Latin was broken,
though scholarly writings in Latin, especially in philosophy, medi-
cine, and law, continued to appear throughout the eighteenth century
and well into the nineteenth. It is still, of course, used extensively by
the Roman Catholic Church.

The other great rival to German was French. In the courtly
society of the twelfth and thirteenth centuries and again from the
late sixteenth century to our own day many French words and
phrases have entered the German language; and we shall deal with
these in a later chapter.[1] Our present concern is with the rivalry of
French and German as languages. French culture had acquired such
high prestige in western Europe, especially during and after the reign
of Louis XIV (1643–1715), that fashionable court circles in the
German territorial capitals, and indeed the German upper classes
generally, came to admire and imitate everything French, architecture and theatre, literature and music, clothes and social manners,
and even to consider French a more suitable language in polite
society than German. At Frederick the Great's court, for example,
German was relegated to the position of an uncouth language un-
suited for the arts; 'L'allemand est pour les soldats et pour les
chevaux,' wrote Voltaire from Potsdam in 1750. And Goethe's
sister Cornelia kept her diary and wrote to her friends in French.
With the flourishing German classical literature, however, and the
patriotic hostility to Napoleon this threat to the status of German
passed, though French remained as the language of certain aristo-
cratic circles until well through the nineteenth century.

The final establishment of New High German as a literary language
in a standard unified form was the work chiefly of scholars and poets.
In the later sixteenth century grammarians had begun to reduce the
German language to rule; but the first influential figure belongs to
the early seventeenth century. He is Martin Opitz (1597–1639), who
in his *Aristarchus sive de contemptu linguae teutonicae* (1617) wrote
(in Latin!) a passionate defence of his native tongue and whose *Buch
von der deutschen Poeterey* (1624) set the subject matter, metre,
language, and style for German poetry for well over a hundred years.
Taking the language of both Luther and the chanceries (especially

[1] See pp. 75f., 79.

the imperial chancery) as his guide he laid down rules for grammatical points (e.g. the use of unaccented final *e*, the past indicative form of strong verbs) and for the purity and correctness of the vocabulary; at the same time he set the pattern for the elaborately complex, decorative, elevated, and learned style which separates German baroque poetry from the language of everyday use. More than a century later Gottsched and Bodmer, for all their differences of opinion, still looked to Opitz as their guide.

In 1629 Opitz became a member of the *Fruchtbringende Gesellschaft*, a society founded in Weimar in 1617 on the model of the Florentine *Accademia della Crusca* 'zu Erhaltung und Fortpflantzung aller Ritterlichen Tugenden, Aufrichtung und Vermehrung Teutschen wohlgemeinten Vertrauens und sonderlich daß unsere bishero verlassene, verachtete und in letzten Zügen ligende Teutschinne sich erholend, ihre nohtleidende Kinder, Teutsches Geblüts und Gemüts, in etwas sich ermuntern.'[1] It was followed by similar societies elsewhere, including the *Deutschgesinnte Genossenschaft* of Hamburg (1642), the *Hirten- und Blumenorden an der Pegnitz* of Nuremberg (1644) and the *Elbschwanenorden* of Lübeck (1658). These societies, known as *Sprachgesellschaften*, united noblemen, poets, and scholars in pursuit of a wide variety of patriotic, ethical, and cultural aims; their cultivation of German language and literature was by no means their only activity. In the field of language they defended German against its rivals Latin and French, advocated a unified language (with a unified pronunciation), and sought to develop the beauties of German and preserve its purity. Their protests against the excessive use of foreign words and their efforts to replace these by native German ones represent the beginning of a movement which has continued with fluctuating strength ever since.

Some members of the *Sprachgesellschaften* made notable contributions to the establishment and enrichment of standard German. The *Teutsche Sprachkunst* (1641) and the *Ausführliche Arbeit von der Teutschen Haubt-Sprache* (1663) of Justus Georg Schottel, a member of the Weimar and Nuremberg societies, encouraged the acceptance of unified rules of spelling and replaced Latin grammatical terms with

---

[1] 'for the preservation and propagation of all knightly virtues, the establishment and increase of well intentioned confidence among German people and especially that, as our Germania, hitherto neglected, despised and lying *in extremis*, returns to health, her suffering children of German blood and spirit may find therein some measure of encouragement.' (C. G. von Hille, *Der Teutsche Palmbaum*, Nuremberg 1647, p. 10, slightly adapted.)

German ones. For Schottel, standard German was principally a written language, and though he accepted Luther and the chanceries as guides, he insisted that this literary language should be based, not on any dialect or regional language, but on the usage of 'learned, wise and clever men'. Georg Philipp Harsdörffer, the founder of the Nuremberg society, provided a practical guide to the handling of the poetical language in his *Poetischer Trichter, die Teutsche Dicht- und Reimkunst, ohne Behuf der lateinischen Sprache, in sechs Stunden einzugießen*[1] (1647–53). Meanwhile writers of all kinds, both members and non-members of the *Sprachgesellschaften*, were exploiting the resources of the language and adding to the riches of its vocabulary. In the last connection Friedrich von Logau and Philipp von Zesen perhaps deserve special mention.

At the end of the seventeenth century and in the first half of the eighteenth, many distinguished scholars contributed to the establishment of the standard language, including Christian Thomasius, Gottfried Wilhelm Leibniz, the first of the great German philosophers, and Christian Wolff. The outstanding figure, however, is undoubtedly Johann Christoph Gottsched (1700–66), who wrote and taught for over forty years in Leipzig. His literary theories were severely – and rightly – criticized in his own day; but his *Deutsche Sprachkunst* (1748) and other writings on language found greater favour as authoritative works. With complete assurance and much good sense he laid down rules for grammatical and stylistic usage in German. Like Schottel he regarded literary German as independent of any dialect or region. But in practice he advocated the East Middle German standard; and it was largely through his authority that the south finally accepted this form of German as the standard one. Even his Swiss critics, Johann Jacob Bodmer and Johann Jacob Breitinger, agreed with him in this – in theory, though not always in practice. Gottsched's model was closely followed by Johann Christoph Adelung in his *Vollständige Anweisung zur deutschen Orthographie* (1788) and his *Versuch eines vollständigen grammatisch-kritischen Wörterbuchs der hochdeutschen Mundart* (1774–86), the first great dictionary of standard German.[2]

The final stage in the establishment of German as a literary langu-

---

[1] 'Poetical Funnel for the Infusion of the Art of German Poetry and Rhyme in Six Hours without the Aid of the Latin Tongue.'
[2] Adelung's dictionary, with its normative function, is more akin to the *Dictionnaire de l'Académie Française* than to the *Oxford English Dictionary*.

age and of East Middle German as the standard was the emergence of the great poets and writers of the later eighteenth century. Klopstock and Lessing, Herder and Wieland, Goethe and Schiller all used the East Middle German standard – and all enriched and developed it in their different ways. By the end of the eighteenth century there could be no doubt that German was one of the great literary languages of the world.

The patriotic philosophers and poets of the early nineteenth century had certainly no doubt. Johann Gottlieb Fichte proclaimed in his *Reden an die deutsche Nation* (1808) that the German language, the German character and political mission were more valuable than those of the French. Poets like Fouqué and Arndt protested at the French influence still evident in the language. What is more important, the Romantic movement with its characteristic interest in the Middle Ages led scholars – not for the first time but now more systematically – to study the earlier stages of German and to inaugurate the tradition of Germanic and comparative philology which was one of the great achievements of the nineteenth-century German universities and from which other countries have learnt much. Its greatest monument is the *Deutsches Wörterbuch*, which Jakob and Wilhelm Grimm began to publish in 1852; with all its faults it is one of the great storehouses of information about the German language.[1]

By the late nineteenth century the spread of education and the immense increase in printed matter of all kinds made the need for uniformity in spelling a pressing one. Conferences were held, government directives issued. These were incorporated in Konrad Duden's *Vollständiges Orthographisches Wörterbuch der deutschen Sprache*, first published in 1880; this handbook (now entitled *Rechtschreibung der deutschen Sprache und der Fremdwörter*), though criticized in detail and now appearing in separate eastern and western editions, is regarded as the standard reference book. German spelling is much less chaotic than English; but it is still not uniform and further reforms are being discussed.

Until late in the nineteenth century the standard language was regarded chiefly as a written language. The colloquial speech of educated people, though separate from the local dialects and tending more and more to conform to the literary language, retained many

---

[1] The Grimms' dictionary was not completed until 1960. Its early volumes are much in need of revision and this is now being done.

features of local dialect pronunciation in the various regions. The disadvantages of this were keenly felt by actors, who wished to be acceptable and intelligible in theatres throughout the German-speaking world. A commission of university professors and representatives of the *Deutscher Bühnenverein* (German Theatrical Society), meeting in Berlin in 1898, led to the publication of Theodor Siebs' *Deutsche Bühnenaussprache* (1898), in which for various linguistic, social, and political reasons, north German pronunciation is given preference over southern usage. This handbook has largely been accepted as authoritative by the theatres and, to a lesser extent, by the film industry and the main broadcasting stations; and by the title of its latest edition, *Deutsche Hochsprache, Bühnenaussprache*, it claims to represent the ideal pronunciation for all users of standard German. But the strong regional traditions, the political division between eastern and western Germany[1] and the separate existence of Austria and Switzerland make the establishment of a uniform pronunciation unlikely in practice – and perhaps not even very desirable.

Finally, what of the future? How will the German-speaking area and the political and social groupings of German speakers change? Will it be shown that literary movements such as expressionism or poltical experiences such as the National Socialist regime or the division between East and West have had lasting and notable effects on the language? Will the dialects[2] disappear? Will spelling reforms be introduced? Will the use of the genitive case and the subjunctive mood continue to decrease, as seems to be the case today? Will the present tendency to more and longer compound words and to growing abstraction, with a loss of vividness and plasticity, continue? Language is subject to so many varied and incalculable influences that it would be idle to speculate. We turn instead in the following chapters to the history of German vocabulary and then of its sounds, forms, and syntax.

FOR FURTHER READING

August Langen, 'Deutsche Sprachgeschichte vom Barock bis zur Gegenwart', in *Deutsche Philologie im Aufriß*, 2nd edn., Vol. 1, cols. 931–1396

---

[1] For some examples of the effects of this division on the vocabulary, see p. 90, note 1.

[2] Dialects are much more vigorously alive today in Germany than in England, though the influence of the standard language on them is strong. Here, however, we concentrate on the history of the standard literary language, the type of German which foreign students of German know best and need to study most fully.

A short history of the German language

Eric A. Blackall, *The emergence of German as a literary language 1700–1775*, 1959

William E. Collinson, *The German language today: its patterns and historical background*, 1953

Lutz Mackensen, *Die deutsche Sprache unserer Zeit: zur Sprachgeschichte des 20. Jahrhunderts*, 1956

Part II

CHAPTER 7

The German vocabulary: word formation

As human society has developed from its earlier, more primitive state to the advanced civilizations of today, men have learnt to analyse their own processes of body and mind and their natural environment in ever greater detail and to control and use natural forces for their own ends. Philosophers, prophets, and artists have given men deeper insight into religion and morals, human emotions, and the life of society. Men have organized themselves in groups such as families, clans, and nations and have developed elaborate systems of law and political and social institutions. Trade and industry have played an ever increasing part in their lives. This long process has been haphazard and its various aspects have taken place at vastly different speeds. There is no direct and steady progression from false-hood to truth, from the dug-out canoe to the space capsule, from the cave-man family to the modern industrial state. What is clear, however, is that men's ideas in the course of the long centuries have grown more and more complex and varied; and that is what chiefly concerns us here.

Every new idea – every new philosophical concept or political institution, every new discovery or process or machine – has involved a change in human language. In each community words have had to be found to represent the new ideas and to convey them to other members of the community. This has been a continuous process; and at every stage the language has kept pace – though often, indeed, imperfectly – with the growth of ideas. This close association between the language of a community and its ideas makes a language a record and mirror of the community's history and experience; and a detailed knowledge of a community's language, more particularly of its vocabulary, at a particular stage of history (or pre-history) is a fairly accurate guide to the community's level of civilization and to the extent and variety of its interests at that particular period.

This process of expansion in the vocabulary has been accompanied by some losses. Old ideas – institutions, customs, tools, attitudes – become obsolete and are abandoned; and the words which represent them fall into disuse – or, often, are adapted to new uses. Or a more fashionable word is substituted for an older one (*Onkel* replaces *Oheim*). Or again, as men have learned to think more abstractly, they have avoided unnecessary words. Certain African languages, for example, have different words for cows of different colours; at a later stage of civilization the need is felt for a generic term for 'cow'.[1] But such losses, though their extent is often difficult to assess for the oldest periods, seem to be small compared with the enormous expansion of vocabulary which has taken place.

With these general considerations in mind we may turn to our survey of German vocabulary. As our starting-point we take the vocabulary of the Indo-European parent language. Here we must proceed with some caution. Indo-European, as we have seen,[2] is not documented and has been reconstructed by comparative methods; and in the field of vocabulary there is much uncertainty. We do not know, for example, how many words have simply disappeared without leaving a trace in any documented language. Again, if a word appears only in a small number of languages, how can we tell whether it has always been confined to these languages or whether it was once part of the parent vocabulary? Conversely, if a word appears in a large number of languages, can we be sure (as we usually assume) that it belonged to the parent language? It is always possible that it spread from one group of languages to others at a later stage. Finally, even if we can say with confidence that a word belonged to the Indo-European vocabulary, it is quite likely that it has changed its meaning and that we cannot now say what it originally meant. Nevertheless it has been possible to reconstruct a considerable part of the Indo-European vocabulary beyond reasonable doubt and to gain some idea of the civilization it reflects. The following outline contains only a small selection of the many German words[3] which have come through Germanic from Indo-European.

---

[1] But even a highly developed language sometimes shows an apparently excessive wealth of vocabulary: Ger. *Klemmer, Kneifer, Zwicker* all mean 'pince-nez'.
[2] See p. 9 ff.
[3] German words are given in their modern standard form unless other forms

The German vocabulary: word formation

The Indo-Europeans, as one might expect, had words for all the main parts of the body (*Haupt, Bauch, Ferse, Zahn, Auge, Ohr, Zunge, Hals, Leib, Arm, Hand, Fuß, Herz, Ader, Niere*) and for common human actions (*gehen, kommen, springen, stehen, sitzen, liegen, schlafen, wachen, essen, sagen, fragen, wissen, wollen, sterben*). They could also describe their natural environment in some detail (*Sonne, Mond, Stern, Tag, Nacht, Dämmer, Licht, Sommer; Felsen, Berg, Meer, Ufer, Welle; Wind, Nebel, Schnee, Eis, Donner, Blitz*). They had domesticated animals (*Rind, Kuh, Ochse, Stier, Sau, Bock; zähmen*), they were familiar, no doubt from hunting, with other wild animals and birds (*Fuchs, Wolf, Bär, Biber, Dachs, Otter, Hirsch; Aar, Geier, Ente, Gans, Schwan, Specht, Star*) and they used animal products for food and other purposes (*Ei, Milch, Fell, Leder, Horn, Wolle, Honig, Wachs; gären, scheren, seihen, weben*). But they also cultivated the land with simple tools (*Egge, Rechen, Schar* 'ploughshare'; *Furche; säen, mähen, bauen*) to grow crops (*Gerste, Korn, Erbse*) and they were familiar with wild plants, especially with trees (*Fichte, Buche, Esche, Eiche, Ahorn, Birke, Linde*). Their constructional techniques had advanced far beyond primitive savagery. They built houses of wood or wattle with tools (*Holz, Balken, Dach, Diele, Tor, Tür; Beil, Zange, Ahle; bohren, binden, flechten*), they possessed carts and boats (*Achse, Rad, Joch, Deichsel; Ruder*) and they knew one metal, copper (*ehern, Erz*). They had learned to cook with fire (*Feuer, Lohe, Asche; Fladen, Brei, Teig*) and to make mead (*Met*). Their relationships in family and clan were strongly developed (*Vater, Mutter, Bruder, Schwester, Sohn, Tochter, Oheim, Neffe, Vetter, Schwäher, Enkel; Sippe*). As is natural in a community at an early stage of civilization, their vocabulary mainly represented concrete things and situations; but it also reflected more abstract social, legal, moral, and emotional concepts (*Ehe, Bann, Freund, Feind, Gast, Raub; frei, eigen; kiesen, leihen, mahnen, zeihen; Ehre, Ruhm, Lust, Minne; lieb*).[1] It also contained the name of one god, represented in Greek by Zeus (Lat. *Jupiter*, OHG. *Ziu*). The numbers 'one' to 'ten' and 'hundred' go back to Indo-European, which also seems to have had a full complement of personal pronouns and a number of prepositions.

---

are specifically required. Older forms and cognate words in other languages may be found in the etymological dictionaries mentioned in the bibliography, p. 159.

[1] Among such abstract words changes of meaning have been particularly frequent and far-reaching.

A short history of the German language

How did the Germanic peoples, who inherited this kind of vocabulary, supplement and adapt it to keep it adequate to represent the ever-changing ideas of the community? Four courses were open to them: they could invent entirely new words; they could form new words from elements already in the language; they could borrow words from other languages; they could give old words new meanings. The first of these procedures, the creation of new words without reference to existing ones, was, we may suppose, common in the earliest stages of human language; but in the historical period of language it is so rare that it need not concern us further. The other three procedures have been common throughout the history of German and are still very much alive today. The rest of this chapter will examine the first of them, word-formation; and the next two chapters will deal with borrowing and change of meaning.

The formation of new words from elements already present in the language has been characteristic of the Germanic languages throughout their history; and it remains a vigorous feature of German (and English) today.[1] We may distinguish two main types of word-formation, composition (*Zusammensetzung*) and derivation (*Ableitung*). Composition consists in forming new words by combining two (or more) elements each of which also exists as an independent word; *Rathaus* is a compound formed from *Rat* and *Haus*. Derivation consists in forming new words by combining independent words, or their stems, with formative elements which have no independent existence as words; *Maler* is a derivative formed by adding the formative element (in this case the suffix) *-er* to *mal-* (the stem of *malen*).

From a historical point of view this distinction is not a very sharp one. Many of the elements now used to form derivatives once existed as independent words; this, indeed, may be true of all of them. Early Indo-European, as we have seen,[2] probably consisted of simple words which did not change in form but were arranged in different orders to form sentences. Later certain words, whose function was to show relationships between the ideas represented, became less strongly accented and were attached, as prefixes, suffixes, and

---

[1] The German convention of writing long compounds as single words lends some weight to the view that the existence of 'very long words' in German constitutes an important difference between German and English. But this difference should not be exaggerated. To an English speaker *An einem Spätherbstnachmittage* may *look* more formidable than *On a late autumn afternoon*; when the words are *spoken* the difference largely disappears. See also the last paragraph of this chapter, p. 67.

[2] See p. 10.

58

inflexional endings,[1] to the words which carried the principal
meaning. We cannot demonstrate this for Indo-European, since we
can only reconstruct a late form of the language; but the process can
be observed within the historical period of German. In Old and
Middle High German the word *heit* 'nature', 'quality', 'person',
'rank' existed as a separate word, though it was early used as the
second part of compounds: *Freiheit*, OHG. *frīheit*, originally meant
'free state', 'free condition'. Now it exists only as a suffix forming
abstract nouns: *Kühnheit, Sicherheit, Gottheit*. The suffixes *-schaft* and
-tum (*Bruderschaft, Landschaft; Eigentum, Reichtum*) have similar
histories. The OHG. word *līh* meant '(human) body' (modern *Leiche*
'dead body', 'corpse' is closely connected). It early became an
adjectival suffix, meaning 'in the shape of, having the nature of';
göttlich originally meant 'in the form of a god', hence 'divine'. Today
such elements, formerly independent words, are felt and used solely
as derivative elements; and it is therefore possible, for practical
purposes, to keep the distinction between composition and derivation.

A. COMPOSITION

Once a compound has been formed and established it becomes a word
like any other word in the language. It is not, for example, being
continuously re-formed but may preserve in a fossilized form words,
inflexions, or constructions which are now obsolete. *Bräutigam* preserves in its second element an old word for 'man', OHG. *gomo*,
while its first element shows an old form of the genitive singular,
OHG. *brūt*, gen. *brūti*, MHG. *brūt*, gen. *briute*. *Vorhanden* preserves
an old dative plural, *handen*, of MHG. *hant*. *Vergißmeinnicht* reflects
a time when *vergessen* governed the genitive and preserves the old
genitive of the personal pronoun, MHG. *mīn* (now *meiner*).

But compounds, once formed, also develop and function as single
words. There is, for example, a constant tendency in German for
final and other unaccented syllables to be reduced and even to disappear. This has happened in *Nachbar*, MHG. *nāchgebūr*. The second
syllable has entirely disappeared, and the final syllable, instead of
developing into *Bauer*, as the simple word has done, now appears in
the reduced form of *-bar*. Again, compounds are inflected only in
their final element; it is the word as a whole, not its separate elements, which functions syntactically in a sentence: *er trägt Hand-*

[1] Inflexional endings are dealt with in Chapter 12, p. 118 ff.

schuhe, not *er trägt Händeschuhe*! And further, compounds have frequently a meaning which is different from that obtained by combining the meanings of the separate elements of the word. *Großvater* is not a 'tall father' nor is a *Wörterbuch* simply a 'book of words', while one's *Siebensachen* ('goods and chattels') are hardly ever limited to seven! Some acquire their special meaning from the beginning – and have indeed been formed to express that meaning: *Halbinsel* has always meant 'peninsula'. Others acquire it in the course of their further development: *Marschall* goes back to OHG. *marahscalc* 'horse-servant', i.e. 'groom', which later acquired the meaning of 'official in a nobleman's household' and finally its present military meaning. Incidentally, this development of a special meaning is shared by many set phrases. *Der Stille Ozean* is not any quiet ocean, but the Pacific, *rote Rüben* are specifically beetroot, and *Haus und Hof* implies more than just the house and courtyard.

It has long been customary to distinguish between 'real' and 'unreal' compounds (sometimes called 'proper' and 'improper', in German, *eigentliche und uneigentliche*, or *echte und unechte Zusammensetzungen*). In real compounds the first element appears as a bare uninflected word-stem which is combined directly with the second element: *Vaterland, Königreich, Stadtmauer, Bahnhof*. In unreal compounds, on the other hand, the first element has an inflexional ending, often a genitive, and stands in a syntactical relationship to the second element: *Ackersmann, Gottessohn, Blumenbeet, Kinderstube, Händedruck*. So widespread has this second type become that the genitive ending, particularly the *-s*, often appears where it is grammatically out of place: *Weihnachtsbaum, Universitätsprofessor, weisheitsvoll*. The difference is neatly illustrated in *Landmann* 'countryman, farmer' and *Landsmann* 'compatriot' (where a difference in meaning has developed parallel to the formal difference).

The distinction between real and unreal compounds is a very old one. It is very probable that compounds of the first type were formed in Indo-European before inflexional endings were developed. Those of the second type – or at least the models for them, for many compounds are formed by analogy – arose at a later stage from syntactically related groups of words. A common group was one in which a substantive governed a genitive preceding it. Until the Middle High German period the genitive could be inserted between the governing substantive and its article or adjective (MHG. *der sanges meister, diu swære gotes zuht*) or the genitive with *its* dependent article or adjective could be placed before the governing substantive (MHG. *der muoter rede*). Both of these patterns are forerunners of compounds, though in some cases it is hardly possible to say which; *Gottessohn* almost certainly comes from *der gotes sun*, but does *Kinderstube* come from *diu kinder stube* or *der kinder stube*?

But though the origins of real and unreal compounds are different, both types are found in the earliest documents and both still serve as models for modern compounds: *Gasherd* and *Weltraumfahrt* as well as *Volkswagen* and *Elektrizitätswerk*. To call one type 'real' or 'proper' and the other 'unreal' or 'improper' is quite misleading; the second type is as real or proper as the first. They might be called 'primary' and 'secondary', as C. T. Carr suggests; this would avoid the suggestion that the second type is somehow inferior to the first.

Another and probably more useful way of classifying compounds is to take compound substantives and adjectives, compound verbs, and compound particles separately.

1. *Compound substantives*[1] *and adjectives.* We may distinguish three main types:

(*a*) Determinative compounds (by far the largest group): in these the second element is 'determined' or made more precise by the first. The range of pattern is very wide. The first element may be a substantive (*Vaterland, Apfelbaum, Ratsherr, blutrot, wasserdicht, segensreich*), an adjective (*Großvater, Hochmut, Schwarzbrot; altklug, hellblau, halbbewußt*), a verb (*Schreibzeug, Schlafzimmer, Sparkasse; treffsicher, merkwürdig, knitterfrei*) or some other part of speech (*Vorstadt, Umwelt, Gegenteil, Mißerfolg*).

(*b*) Copulative compounds: the two elements are linked in apposition, without the one's limiting or determining the other. Indo-European seems to have had many examples; but they are rare in the early periods of the Germanic languages, the best examples being the cardinal numbers from thirteen to nineteen. The obscure *sunufatarungo* of the *Hildebrandslied* – meaning perhaps '(the people of?) son and father' – may contain an example. Modern examples are more common: *Prinzregent, Werwolf, Schleswig-Holstein; taubstumm, naßkalt, schwarzweißrot*.

(*c*) Possessive compounds: the person or thing designated is implied indirectly (hence the alternative term 'exocentric' for this

[1] For explanatory compounds see p. 73, note 1.

group); what is named directly is a thing or quality possessed by the implied subject. *Rotbart* implies '(a person having a) red beard'. Other examples are: *Dummkopf, Freigeist, Lästerzunge; barfuß.* Similar to these are the so-called imperative compounds, which have developed from short imperative sentences, *Fürchtegott, Vergiß-meinnicht.*

2. *Compound verbs* present far less variety than compound substantives and adjectives. The first element may be either an adverbial particle or a substantive or adjective. We distinguish between inseparable compounds, in which the two elements remain together in all types of sentence (*Ich umgehe das Haus; ich habe das Haus umgangen*), and separable compounds, in which the elements are separated in certain circumstances (*Ein Gerücht geht um; . . . ist umgegangen; . . . soll umgehen*). In inseparable compounds the word accent falls on the verbal element, in separable compounds it falls on the first element.

Certain particles (*über-, unter-, hinter-, durch-, um-, wieder-* and *wider-*), and the adjective *voll-* may form either separable or inseparable compounds. When the same particle and verb form both a separable and an inseparable compound, the formal difference is often accompanied by a difference in meaning or syntactical usage: *Der Fährmann setzt den Wanderer über* ('ferries across'), *er übersetzt ein Buch* ('translates'); *er zieht den Faden durch* ('pulls . . . through'), *er durchzieht das Land* ('passes through'); *ich fahre nur durch* (intransitive), *ich durchfahre die ganze Stadt* (transitive). Sometimes, however, the difference in meaning is hardly perceptible: *ich bohre das Brett durch, ich durchbohre das Brett.* In practice a good deal of uncertainty exists; Duden gives, for example, *wiederhólen* but *wíderspiegeln, wíderklingen* but *widerspréchen.*

Separable verbal compounds are formed with *ab-, an-, auf-,* etc.; *hin-, her-, dar-,* and their compounds; *abwärts-, einwärts-,* etc.; *zusammen-, entgegen-;* and several others: *abschreiben, entgegenkommen.* Examples are so common that the list can very easily be added to.

Verbs with a substantive or adjective as first element are comparatively few in number. Most are separable compounds: *heimfahren, teilnehmen, standhalten; freigeben, hochschätzen, festbinden;* but a few are inseparable: *gewährleisten, liebäugeln; wehklagen, ratschlagen, langweilen.* The last three, like many in this group, are really deriva-

tives from compound substantives – *Wehklage*, etc. – and all are
accented on the first element.

3. *Compound particles*. These comprise adverbs, prepositions, and
conjunctions, and have developed in many different ways. We give
a few examples, without analysing them: *dahin, nachher, obenan;
immerhin, obwohl, überaus; mitunter, widerum; abhanden, beinahe,
bergan, geradeaus, keineswegs, stufenweise, überall, umsonst, vor-
gestern, zufolge; allzeit, diesmal*; and many others.

B. DERIVATION

Derivatives may be divided into those formed with prefixes and those
formed with suffixes. Prefixes in their turn may be divided into those
used with substantives and adjectives and those used with verbs.
The Germanic languages once possessed several prefixes used with
substantives and adjectives; and some survive in fossilized form, as
in *Antlitz*.[1] But only two are still in active use:

un-: essentially expresses negation and may be prefixed to most
adjectives (*unfreundlich, unrecht, unwahrscheinlich*) including participles (*unvergessen, unerkannt*) and some substantives (*Undank,
Unglück*). With some substantives it expresses an undesirable or
intensified variant of the basic idea: *Unwetter, Unkosten, Unmenge.*

ur-: originally this indicated the cause or source of something;
it now means 'original, primitive': *Urzeit, Urtext, Urwald; urger-
manisch.* With adjectives it is often merely emphatic: *uralt, urkom-
isch.*

To these we may add *erz-*, from Greek *archi-*, which reached
German in Latin words like *archiepiscopus* which becomes German
Erzbischof. It is used in a wider, non-technical sense to express
emphasis in words of pejorative meaning: *Erzbösewicht, erzdumm.*

Derivative verbs are formed with the following prefixes:[2]

be- (related to *bei*) expresses the strengthening or generalization or
direction of the action: *bedecken, begießen, bemalen.* An important
use is in the formation of transitive verbs: *betrachten, besteigen,
bedrohen, bestehen;* but it also occurs in intransitive ones: *beruhen,*

[1] See footnote 1 on p. 64.
[2] These are unaccented and inseparable prefixes. The so-called separable prefixes are really the first element of compounds; cf. p. 62.

behagen, bleiben. In *bleiben* it is shortened and hardly recognizable.

er-[1] has two main senses, the beginning of the action (*erblühen, erschrecken*) or its completion (*erschlagen, ertrinken, erhören*); but its sense often seems quite vague (*erwidern, erstaunen, erlauben*).

ent-[1] has the sense of doing the opposite of what the simple verb expresses (*entfalten, entfesseln, entkleiden*) or separation (*entführen, entlassen, enthaupten*). But again a specific meaning is often difficult to find (*entsprechen, entgelten*). Before *f*, *ent-* appears as *emp-* (*empfangen, empfinden*).

ge- (cognate with Latin *cum*) may express union, togetherness: *gerinnen* 'coagulate'. (Hence its use, with the Germanic suffix *-ja/-jo*, to form collectives and similar substantives: *Gebirge, Geselle, Geflügel*.) It also expresses the beginning or completion of the action in verbs (its perfective sense); hence it early came to be the sign of the past participle, a usage which has been generalized in the modern language without regard to meaning. This perfective sense is seen in MHG. *gesitzen* 'sit down' in contrast to *sitzen* 'be sitting'. Only a small number of verbs with *ge-* survive: *gedenken, gebieten, geschehen*, etc. Before *l* it is sometimes contracted: *glauben*.

ver- corresponds to three Latin prefixes *per-, por-, pro-*. The forms are clearly distinguished in Gothic (*faír-, faúr-, fra-*) but already confused in Old High German. Gothic *fra-* 'away' is reflected in *vernichten, verrechnen, verreisen*, Gothic *faúr-* 'in front of, past' in *verdecken, verhüllen, verbieten*; but few such correspondences can be observed in modern derivatives. *ver-* seems often to be merely emphatic (*vereinigen, verfinstern*) or to serve as a means of making verbs (*verarmen, verschönern*).

zer- appears in Old High German first as *za-* (*zi-, ze-*). The modern form with *r* has been variously explained, either as a compound with *er-*, or as formed by analogy with *ver-* or as the original form, of which *za-* is a shortened form. It implies violent action, often one of separating or breaking in pieces: *zerschmettern, zerbrechen, zerreißen, zerbleuen*.

miß- 'wrong', 'false', occupies an anomalous position. It no longer exists as a separate word and has some of the qualities of an inseparable prefix (*mißversteh mich nicht*, not *versteh mich nicht miß*!), yet it is sometimes accented (*mißverstehen*) and is sometimes treated

---

[1] *er-* is the unaccented form of *ur-*, which, being accented in substantives, has retained its full vowel. *ent-* is similarly related to the now fossilized prefix *ant-* (*Antwort, Antlitz*).

64

as a separable prefix (*mißzuverstehen*). In these cases its old status as a separate word is reflected.

We turn finally to derivatives made with suffixes. Here we must confine our attention to some of the suffixes which are still most active in producing new words, leaving aside the many which were once active but now survive only in a fossilized form (e.g. the agent-suffix OHG. -*o*, seen as -*e* in *Bote*; or the abstract suffix OHG. -*ī*, seen as -*e* in *Länge*; or the abstract suffix Gmc. -*ti*, seen as *t* in *Macht, Tat*). We shall deal separately with suffixes forming substantives, those forming adjectives and those forming verbs. Some of the suffixes contain or once contained an *i* and cause a change in the vowel[1] of the original word (*Hund: Hündin*); but there is not complete consistency in this.

Diminutives are formed with -*chen* and *lein*. The geographical distribution of these in the past is not entirely clear, but both are current in the modern standard language: *Mäuschen, Liebchen, Büchlein, Kindlein* (or *Kindchen*!) Words denoting female occupations, titles, animals, and the like are formed with -*in*: *Lehrerin, Doktorin, Hündin*. The agent or the instrument is often formed with -*er*, a suffix developed from Latin -*ārius*, which has replaced a number of Germanic agent suffixes: *Schneider, Bäcker, Lügner; Bohrer, Fernsprecher, Staubsauger*.

Abstract nouns are made with various suffixes. The most common are -*ung* (*Nahrung, Bewegung, Entsagung*) and -*heit*, -*schaft*, -*tum*, which were once independent words[2] (*Schönheit, Vergangenheit; Bruderschaft, Gefangenschaft; Reichtum, Christentum*). Less common are -*sal* (*Mühsal, Schicksal*), -*nis* (*Kenntnis, Gefängnis, Finsternis, Bündnis*)[3] and -*ei*, developed from Latin -*ia* and Old French -*ie*, but now used with native German words (*Malerei, Arznei*). Some words formed with -*ei* or its expanded forms -*erei*, -*elei* imply disapproval: *Schwärmerei, Schmeichelei, Frömmelei*.[4]

Among adjectival suffixes -*en* means 'made of'. Its Old High

---

[1] For these vowel changes see p. 97, point (13) (fracture) and p. 106 ff, point (6) (umlaut).
[2] See p. 58 f.
[3] Since -*nis* represents the OHG. feminine -*nissa*, -*nissī* or the neuter -*nissi* words in -*nis* are either feminine or neuter.
[4] Many of the 'abstract' nouns have acquired a second, concrete meaning (which may indeed be their only meaning in the modern language). For example MHG. *gevancnisse* meant 'capture, captivity'; today *Gefängnis* means only 'prison'.

A short history of the German language

German form -*īn* (*guldīn*) survives in only a few words (*golden, seiden, eichen*). The form -*ern*, which probably arose by analogy with forms like *silbern*, (OHG. *silbarīn*) is now commoner: *gläsern, steinern*, even *hölzern, eisern* (despite OHG. *hulzīn, īsīn*). Other common adjective suffixes are:

-*ig* (perhaps the commonest adjective suffix): *feurig, nötig, wollig, frömmig*.

-*isch* 'pertaining to': *kindisch, modisch*, and in contracted form: *deutsch, hübsch*.

-*lich*, whose history we have already mentioned:[1] *lieblich, vortrefflich, kindlich* (contrast *kindisch* above).

-*bar* 'bearing, producing' (connected with *gebären*): *fruchtbar, wunderbar*.

-*haft* 'possessing, equipped with' (cognate with Latin *captus*): *vorteilhaft, fehlerhaft*.

In many derivatives with these suffixes the original sense has been lost and derivatives are formed simply by analogy: *trinkbar, hörbar; fabelhaft, musterhaft*.

Many new verbs are formed from substantives, adjectives, and other verbs[2] without derivative suffixes by the addition of inflexions to the basic word: *Rost – rosten; Trost – trösten*. In some such verbs, as these examples show, the change causes a modification of the stem vowel; in others the vowel is unchanged. Why is this? Weak verbs – and with few exceptions new verbs have been weak – fall into three classes, whose infinitive in Old High German ended in -*en* (< Gmc. *-*jan*), -*ōn* and -*ēn*. The *-*jan* caused modification of the stem vowel and this remained when the distinctions between the three classes disappeared in Middle High German. Since then new verbs have been formed either with modification of the vowel – the largest number – or without it.

Of verbal suffixes perhaps the most active has been -*ieren*, which developed from the Old French ending *ier* and has produced many, perhaps too many, new verbs since the twelfth century, from *addieren, marschieren, hofieren* to *amerikanisieren* or *shampooieren*.

[1] See p. 59.
[2] Verbs formed from other verbs are often so-called 'factitive' verbs, i.e. they have the meaning 'to make (someone) do something'. They are normally formed from the past stem of the original verb. Thus *führen*, 'to make go', hence 'to lead', is formed from *fuhr*, the past tense of *fahren* 'to go'.

C. ABBREVIATIONS AND LONG WORDS

All the methods of word-formation we have been discussing have been used fairly continuously throughout the history of German. There is no room in a brief introduction to estimate which methods have been most popular and characteristic in each period; indeed preliminary studies for such an estimate hardly exist for most periods. Instead we shall end with a brief look at a peculiarly modern type of word-formation, the abbreviated word. The tendency itself is not new; OHG. *sarc* (NHG. *Sarg*) represents Latin *sarcophagus*, and *Ober* (for *Oberkellner*) or *Kilo* (for *Kilogramm*) are long established. But the speed of modern life, the increasing number and complexity of inventions and institutions, and the vast growth in printed matter of all kinds have led to more and more abbreviations (*Auto, Photo, Kino*) combined with a tendency to shorten words by combining into a new word the initial letters or syllables of the component parts of a longer word or phrase. Nor is this so-called *Akü-sprache* (*Abkürzungssprache*) confined to German; readers may easily supply English parallels to many of the following examples. *BGB* (*Bürgerliches Gesetzbuch*), *CDU* (*Christlich-Demokratische Union*), *DDR* (*Deutsche Demokratische Republik*), *EKD* (*Evangelische Kirche in Deutschland*) or *VW* (*Volkswagen*) are perhaps not words at all, since they are pronounced according to the names of the letters; and the same is partly true of *D-Zug* (*Durchgangszug*) or *U-Boot* (*Unterseeboot*). But this can hardly be maintained with respect to *Flak* (*Fliegerabwehrkanone*) or *Nazi* (*Nationalsozialist*; with its derivative *nazistisch*), *Leica* (*Leitz-Camera*) or *Hapag* (*Hamburg-Amerikanische Packetfahrt-Actien-Gesellschaft*) or *Ufa* (*Universum-Film-Aktien-gesellschaft*) or *Gestapo* (*Geheime Staatspolizei*).

Some observers have detected in modern German a tendency to form longer words. There is some truth in this, as words like *Arbeitslosenversicherung* or *Kleinrentnerfürsorge* bear witness. Yet the *Aküsprache* serves as an antidote, and in practice excessively long words are hardly ever met with. The famous *Donaudampfschiff-fahrtsgesellschaftskapitän* is a rarity (or perhaps a joke)[1] and a *Kernwaffenversuchseinstellungsabkommen* is speedily transformed into something like an *Atom-Stop-Vertrag*.

---

[1] *The Donau-Dampfschiffahrts-Gesellschaft* refers to itself in print thus (with hyphens) or as *DDSG*!

FOR FURTHER READING

Charles T. Carr, *Nominal compounds in Germanic*, 1939
Walter Henzen, *Deutsche Wortbildung*, 3rd edn., 1965
Wolfgang Meid, *Wortbildungslehre*, 1967 (Sammlung Göschen, No. 1218 a/b)

CHAPTER 8

The German vocabulary: borrowing

A. GENERAL PRINCIPLES; LOAN-WORDS AND FOREIGN WORDS; LOAN TRANSLATION; BORROWING OF MEANING

The second important way of enriching the vocabulary is by borrowing words from other languages. Like most linguistic communities,
the speakers of German have not developed in isolation from the rest
of mankind but have been in contact – political and social, cultural
and commercial – with a wide variety of other linguistic communities.
As a result the German language has been influenced by – and has in
its turn influenced – many other languages in Europe and the rest of
the world. Some of these contacts have been close and lasting and
have influenced German deeply, even leading to changes in its structure; others, being more temporary and superficial, have affected only
this or that detail of the language, mainly in the field of vocabulary.

Throughout its history German has borrowed very large numbers
of foreign words and today it seems more open than ever to such ex-
ternal influences. In what circumstances does such borrowing take
place? In the simplest cases, a name is adopted along with the thing
it represents. The word *tea*, of Chinese origin, became established in
various forms in European languages when Europeans began to use
the Chinese drink. Similarly a new institution, embodying perhaps a
complex group of new ideas and activities, may bring a whole new
technical vocabulary with it. The technical vocabulary of university
life, for example, is still predominantly Latin. But a borrowing may
represent not so much a totally new thing as the discovery of a new
aspect of something which is in itself old. The word *Mauer*, from
Latin *mūrus*,[1] does not indicate that the Germanic peoples did not
build walls until they came into contact with the Romans; indeed

---

[1] Latin words are normally cited in their classical literary forms though they
were often borrowed in a Vulgar Latin, i.e. colloquial, form. Similarly words in
French, English, and other languages are cited in their modern standard forms.

the old word *Wand*, connected with *winden* and meaning originally a 'wall of interlaced twigs', would hardly support such a view. The Romans rather taught them a new method of building with stone and mortar. This example illustrates another principle which underlies many borrowings. Words tend to be borrowed freely from the language of a community which is regarded as superior, whether it be politically dominant, more advanced in the arts or sciences, more highly developed in commerce and industry, or exemplary in some other way. Here fashion can play a leading part. It was chiefly the dominance of French culture and the French language in eighteenth-century Germany which led to the replacement of *Oheim* and *Muhme* by *Onkel* and *Tante*, though no doubt the imprecision of meaning which had developed in the older words also contributed to the change. Finally, as this last example shows, borrowing may be the result of a number of converging circumstances, not all of which we can now know.

A distinction often made in classifying borrowed words is that between loan-words (*Lehnwörter*) and foreign words (*Fremdwörter*). Loan-words, it is often suggested and even explicitly stated, are useful and acceptable, while foreign words are to be avoided and rejected from the language. Such a value judgement would be difficult to maintain; and in any case there is no agreement about definitions. Some writers regard words borrowed before 1500 as loan-words and those borrowed after 1500 as foreign words. Others – perhaps the majority – classify words which have retained their foreign features (spelling, sounds, inflexional forms) as foreign words and those which have been assimilated to German as loan-words. Still others distinguish between words which have produced derivatives (loan-words) and those which have not (foreign words). The word *Parfum*, borrowed from French in the early eighteenth century, would thus be a foreign word according to the first definition – and also according to the second when it is still pronounced with a French nasalized vowel. It presumably has a claim to loan-word status when it is written *Parfüm* and pronounced accordingly, though it still retains its French plural in *-s* as well as having one in *-e*. As to the third definition, *parfümieren* and *Parfümerie* point to the category of loan-words, though the foreign origin of *-ieren* and *-erie* raises further doubts. In any case the distinction has arisen chiefly as an aid in the fight against excessive borrowing and is too rigid and simple to cover the actual facts of the language. All loan-words (which are, after all, also foreign words) tend to become assimilated to German; but the extent and nature of this assimilation is different for different words.

Direct borrowing is not the only way in which foreign languages have influenced German vocabulary. Many words have been formed from native elements or modified in meaning under the direct influence of some foreign word. In some cases the foreign word has simply been translated into German and the resulting German word has taken on the meaning of the foreign word. *Blaustrumpf* was formed on the model of English *bluestocking* and has acquired the meaning of 'women having or affecting literary tastes or learning' from the English word. This process is known as loan translation (*Lehnübersetzung*). Its strictest form involves the literal translation of the foreign word, element by element, as in our example: *blue – blau, stocking – Strumpf*. But the formation may be freer, as in *Vaterland*, corresponding to Latin *patria*, where only *Vater-* is a translation of *patria* (or rather of *patr-*). It is freer still in *Umwelt*, which corresponds to French *milieu* (in the sense of 'environment') but in which neither *Um-* nor *-welt* is a literal translation of any part of the French word. Finally, a German word may acquire the figurative meaning which its equivalent in the foreign language bears, without the formation of a new German word. German *schneiden* has come to mean 'decline to recognize (someone)' under the influence of English *cut*. This last process is known as borrowing of meaning (*Lehnbedeutung*) and like loan translation has played an important part in the development of German vocabulary.

B. BORROWING IN GERMAN; A HISTORICAL SURVEY

Borrowing has taken place from very early times. Indo-European contained some loan-words; the parent form of Ger. *Stern* and Eng. *star* probably had its origin in Babylon. But some of the earliest loan-words which we can identify in German are a group of Celtic words which entered the Germanic language at some time in the last pre-Christian centuries.[1] Whether *Eisen* is one of these is doubtful. Both Celtic and Germanic peoples may well have learned the word from the Illyrians directly, along with a knowledge of iron and its uses; but it is also possible that the knowledge came to the Germanic

[1] See pp. 14 and 20.

71

world via the Celts. In matters of public law and social organization the Germanic tribes seem to have learned from the Celts, as *Amt, Eid, Geisel*, and *Reich* bear witness. *Ger*, 'iron-tipped javelin', probably borrowed its meaning from a related Celtic word. *Welsch*, despite many changes of meaning, contains the Gaulish tribal name Volcae, while many geographical names in German-speaking lands are of Celtic origin: *Rhein, Main, Donau, Mainz, Aschaffenburg, Remagen.*

But this Celtic influence was as nothing compared with the influence exercised by the Romans.[1] Years of warfare followed by centuries in which the Rhenish and Danubian regions were part of the Roman Empire brought the Germanic tribes into close contact with an advanced and complex society; and though in the end they played a leading part in destroying the Empire as a political institution, they remained great admirers of Roman life and culture. The acceptance of Christianity in its Roman form is, in one sense, only the last decisive step in the incorporation of the Germanic barbarians into the tradition of Mediterranean Christian civilization. It is hardly surprising that the Roman language, Latin,[2] the 'lingua franca' of western Europe until the eighteenth century, should have left its mark on German. This influence continued unbroken from the first century to the eighteenth; but three periods are of special importance: the early centuries of the Christian era; the period when the western Germanic tribes were being converted to Christianity (the fifth to the ninth centuries); and the period of humanism and Renaissance (fourteenth to sixteenth centuries). The first of these periods differs from the others in several ways. In the first place it lies before the second sound-shift, which affected the plosive consonants of High German dialects.[3] Latin words borrowed before this change were affected by it – Latin *pilum*: OHG. *pfīl*, NHG. *Pfeil* – so it is often possible, even in the absence of documents, to say approximately when Latin words first entered the German language. (Words borrowed in the second period, on the other hand, sometimes reflect a medieval pronunciation of Latin: *Zelle*, from Lat. *cella*, reflects the medieval pronunciation with *ts*- and not the classical *k*-.) In the second place, while the later Latin loan-words were introduced into German mainly by men of education from written sources, the German barbarians of the first period learned their Latin from soldiers and merchants and local government officials. Some distortion was almost inevitable. Was it, for instance,

[1] See p. 20.   [2] See pp. 14, 28, 32 f..   [3] See p. 23 and for details pp. 112 ff.

72

The German vocabulary: borrowing

Germanic speakers or the legionaries themselves who reduced *via strāta* to *strāta* (*Straße*) or *mīlia* (pl.) *passuum* to *mīla* (sg.; *Meile*) or turned *campus* '(battle-) field' into the battle itself (*Kampf*)? Nevertheless a very large number of words were borrowed with tolerable accuracy. The following small selection may give some idea of the kinds of influence which the Romans exerted on Germanic culture:

War and military activities: *Kampf, Straße, Meile, Pfeil, Wall* (*vallum*); law and administration: *Kaiser* (*Caesar*), *Kerker* (*carcer*), *sicher* (*sēcūrus*), *Zins* (*census*), *Zoll* (*telōneum*); trade: *Kaufmann*[1] (*caupo* 'innkeeper, petty tradesman'), *Markt* (*mercātus*), *Münze* (*monēta*), *Pfund* (*pondo* 'by weight'), *Sack* (*saccus*), *Korb* (*corbis*), *Esel* (*asinus*); agriculture, with new methods, equipment, and plants: *pfropfen* (*propāgāre*), *impfen* (*imputāre*), *Sichel* (*secula*), *Flegel* (*flagellum*), *Kolter* (*culter*), *Pflanze* (*planta*), *Frucht* (*fructus*), *Kirsche* (VL. *ceresia*), *Kohl* (*caulis*), *Pfeffer* (*piper*), *Pfirsich* (*persicum* 'Persian (fruit)'), *Pilz* (*bōlētus*), *Rettich* (*rādix* 'root'); viticulture (previously unknown in the Germanic world): *Wein* (*vīnum*), *Most* (*mustum*), *Essig* (*acētum*), *Kelter* (*calcātūra*), *Trichter* (*trāiectōrium*), *Becher* (VL. *bīcārium*), *Eimer* (*amphora*); building, especially of more elaborate houses in stone and brick: *Ziegel* (*tegula*), *Kalk* (*calx*), *Mauer* (*mūrus*), *Pfeiler* (*pilārium*), *Fenster* (*fenestra*), *Pforte* (*porta*), *Estrich* (medieval Lat. *astricum*), *Kammer* (*camera*), *Keller* (*cellārium*), *Küche* (*coquīna*); domestic life, clothes, furniture, cookery: *Socke* (*soccus*), *Tisch* (*discus*), *Spiegel* (*speculum*), *kochen* (*coquere*), *Schüssel* (*scutella*), *Pfanne* (*patina*), *Kessel* (*catīnus*), *Mühle* (*molīna*), *Semmel* (*simila*). Names of Roman settlements survive in *Köln* (*Colōnia*), *Koblenz* (*Confluentes*), *Konstanz* (*Constantia*) and many other place-names.

The conversion of the Germanic tribes to Christianity and the establishment of the Church, monasteries, and monastic schools account for a second large group of Latin loan-words. The earliest Christian loan-words, however, are of Greek rather than Latin origin and were very probably transmitted in the fifth century by the Goths, who became Christians before the west Germanic tribes and who had close contacts, on the one hand, with the eastern Church and, on the other, with west Germanic tribes, especially the Bavarians, in the Danube region. To this group belong *Kirche* itself

---

[1] This is an example of an explanatory compound, made for the sake of clarity when the first element alone has become unintelligible or ambiguous; other examples are *Maultier* and *Walfisch*, cf. the simple *mule* and *whale* in English.

A short history of the German language

(Gk. *kyriakē* '[house] of the Lord'), *Pfaffe* (*papãs* 'minor cleric'), *Engel* (*ággelos*), *Teufel* (*diábolos*), and *Pfingsten* (*pentēkostē* 'fiftieth [day after Easter]'),[1] as well as *Samstag* (*sábbaton*), which remains the normal word for 'Saturday' in southern Germany.[2]

But of course the great majority of Christian loan-words from the fifth century onwards came from Latin, the universal language of the western Church. Among these are: *Bischof*, *Mönch* (*monachus*), *Nonne* (*nonna*), *Abt* (*abbas*), *Münster* (*monastērium*), *Kloster* (*claustrum*), *Kapelle* (*capella*), *Zelle* (*cella*), *Altar* (*altāre*), *Kreuz* (*crux*), *Kanzel* (*cancelli*), *Messe* (*missa*), *predigen* (*praedicāre*), *Evangelium*, *Psalm* (*psalmus*), *Feier* (*fēria*), *Vesper* (*vespera*), *Almosen*, *opfern* (*operāri*), *Regel* (*rēgula*). Monastic life, gardening, and skilled crafts are reflected in: *Birne* (*pirum*), *Zwiebel* (*cēpulla*), *Rose* (*rosa*), *Lilie* (*lilium*), *Mörtel* (*mortārium*), *Marmel* (*marmor*), *Kamin* (*camīnus*), *Gruft* (*crypta*), *Tiegel* (*tegula*); and the activities of the monastic school and scriptorium are represented by *Schule* (*schola*), *Meister* (*magister*), *dichten* (*dictāre*), *schreiben* (*scrībere*),[3] *Tinte* (*tincta*), *Pergament* (*pergamēnum*, originally from Pergamon), *Brief* (*breve*). A few adjectives – *keusch* (*conscius*), *sauber* (*sōbrius*), perhaps *nüchtern* (*nocturnus*) – were also borrowed. Latin had such a powerful influence in these early centuries that it gave at least one word-forming element to the language: the agent suffix *-ārius*, introduced in words like *molinārius*, OHG. *mulināri*, NHG. *Müller*, has remained the most common agent suffix in German: *Fischer*, *Bäcker*.

Loan-words, however, have one great drawback; for a short time at least they are understood only by those who already know something of the foreign language, though no doubt they soon gain currency simply as words denoting something new even among

---

[1] These must be distinguished from words, such as *Bischof* and *Almosen*, whose origin is ultimately Greek but which reached German via Latin (*episcopus*, *eleēmosyna*).

[2] The other names for days of the week have quite different origins. *Sonntag*, *Montag*, *Donnerstag*, *Freitag* are loan translations of *Sōlis dies*, *Lūnae dies*, *Jovis dies*, *Veneris dies*, Jupiter and Venus being replaced by the Germanic Donar (= Thor) and Fria. *Dienstag* (*Martis dies*) contains *Thinxus*, a title given in the Lower Rhine region to Mars as protector of the *thing* or assembly of the people. *Mittwoch* is a loan translation of *media hebdomas* 'middle (of the) week'. *Sonnabend*, the northern word for 'Saturday', OHG. *sunnūn āband*, was probably modelled on the Old English *sunnan æfen*, a shortened form of **sunnandæges æfen*, 'vigil before Sunday', used by English missionaries.

[3] Writing of a kind, the scratching of (runic) letters on wood or stone, was known to the Germanic people before the monks taught them Latin writing; the verbs used to describe this process were *reißen* and *ritzen* (cf. English *write*). *Schreiben* implies the writing of connected texts on parchment with a pen. For details of this development see Chapter 4, pp. 27 and 28.

74

speakers who know nothing of their original languages. It is perhaps significant that scholars and missionaries, while being on the whole content to use Latin words for persons, things, and activities, were at great pains to express the theological and moral concepts of Christianity in native German words which might allow new converts from paganism to grasp at least something of the meaning of the new religion. This accounts for a great many loan translations of various degrees of strictness – *Mitleid* (*compassio*), *Gewissen* (*conscientia*), *Wohltat* (*beneficium*), *Vorsehung* (*prōvidentia*), *Übermut* (*superbia*), *Herr* (*senior*), *Weihrauch* (*incensum*) – as well as for many examples of borrowed meaning – *Heiland* (*salvātor*), *Beichte* (*confessio*), *Buße* (*poenitentia*), *Hölle* (*infernum*). These latter, which already had an established pagan meaning, must surely have caused some ambiguity, at least for a time. Not all such inventions were successful. In many instances two translations were proposed for the same Latin term; one of these has become generally accepted and the other has disappeared: *mitleiden* (*compati*) has been preferred to OHG. *elandolēn*, *Heiland* to *neriend*, *Erlösung* (*redemptio*) to *erlōsida*, and *der heilige Geist*[1] (*spiritus sanctus*) to *der wīho ātum*. In other cases the German term has been replaced by the Latin word: OHG. *forasago* and *gotspel* have yielded to *Prophet* and *Evangelium*. The forces at work in this process of acceptance and rejection are often very obscure.[2]

The development of chivalrous and courtly culture in the twelfth century exposes German to a new influence. Now French culture, with its stress on the arts and on the refinements of social life and manners, sets the fashion, German literature draws heavily on poets such as Chrétien de Troyes, and it is therefore hardly surprising to find that the literary language of the period is full of French words reflecting both the warlike pursuits of knighthood and the more peaceful and cultivated activities of the court. Many have survived into modern German: *Palast* (*palais*), *Kastell* (OF. *castel*, mod. *château*), *Lanze* (*lance*), *Banner* (*bannière*), *Panzer* (OF. *pancier*), *Turnier* (OF. *tornei*, mod. *tournoi*), *Abenteuer* (*aventure*), *Reim* (*rime*), *Flöte* (*flûte*), *Melodie* (*mélodie*), *Note* (*note*; or Lat. *nota*?), *tanzen* (*danser*), *Preis* (*prix*), *fein* (*fin*), *falsch* (OF. *fals*, mod. *faux*), *klar* (*clair*), *rund* (*rond*); many others disappeared again as chivalrous

[1] *Der heilige Geist*, like *Sonnabend* above and *gotspel* below, is closely modelled on the Old English term used by English missionaries.
[2] For the third main period of Latin influence see p. 78.

culture declined: *tjoste* (OF. *juste*) 'single combat on horseback', *gabelōt* (*gavelot*) 'short hunting spear', *garzun* (*garçon*) 'page-boy'.

French also provided a number of word-forming suffixes at this period. One of these, *-lei*, was an independent word in French (*ley* 'kind') and still in Middle High German; modern forms like *mancherlei, allerlei, zweierlei* still show their origin in a genitive phrase ('of many kinds', etc.). Another suffix, *-ei*, introduced as *-ie* (*vilanīe* 'uncourtly behaviour'), is now used freely with native words: *Zauberei, Jägerei, Bäckerei, Liebelei*. The verbal suffix *-ieren* (Fr. *-ier*), introduced in French words such as *logieren* (*loger*), *hantieren* (*hanter*) was soon widely used with words of many different origins: *hausieren* (Ger. *Haus*), *probieren* (Lat. *proba*), *trainieren* (Eng. *train*). The highly developed sense of rank and social distinction which is characteristic of courtly society is reflected in the use of the second person plural pronoun *ir* (NHG. *Ihr*) as a formal mode of address to a single person. Though sporadic examples occur earlier, this usage is firmly established under the influence of French, where *vous* was – and is – used in the same way. (The modern use of *Sie* goes back only to the seventeenth century.)

One of the first areas to be affected by French culture and language was the Low Franconian region of the Lower Rhine. Here, for example, *chevalier* in its special meaning of 'knight' was rendered by *riddere, armes* '(coat of) arms' by *wāpen* and *vilain* 'uncourtly person' by *dorpere*. Such was the prestige of this region as a model of chivalrous culture that it became fashionable even in High German regions to 'speak in a Flemish way', *mit der rede vlæmen*.[1] Hence the appearance, in the MHG. literary language, of *ritter* (with double medial consonant), *wāpen* and *dorpære* (both with *-p-*).[2] They survive as *Ritter, Wappen*, and *Tölpel*, while the High German equivalents of the first two, *Reiter* and *Waffe*, have developed other meanings.[3] Along with these come other Low German words such as *ors* (HG. *Roß*), *blīde* 'merry' (Eng. *blithe*), which had no connection with French, as well as the diminutive suffix *-kin* (HG. *-chen*).

In contrast to courtly literature, the language of the mystics shows

---

[1] This fashion was still strong enough to be satirized in *Meier Helmbreht* after 1250.

[2] For the normal development of -p- in High German, see p. 112, point (17).

[3] *Ritter/Reiter* and *Wappen/Waffe* are examples of doublets, i.e. words of different form and meaning which show a common origin. There are many examples in German: *Ziegel/Tiegel* from Latin *tegula*; *Tisch/Diskus* from Lat. *discus*; *Pfalz/Palast/Palais* from Lat. *palatium*, the last two via French in the twelfth and seventeenth centuries respectively.

few loan-words. They were concerned to describe and comment on their experiences in the vernacular; and their valuable contribution to German vocabulary is a large number of derivative and compound words formed with native elements. Yet they inherited a technical vocabulary from their predecessors, who had written in Latin, and many of their new words are thus loan translations: *unaussprechlich* (*ineffābilis*), *Einfluß* (*influxus*), *Eindruck* (*impressio*), *einsehen* (*inspicere*), *beschauen* (*contemplāre*), *Zufall* (*accidens*), and others, such as *gegenwurf* or *vürwurf* (*objectum*), *underwurf* (*subjectum*), which have not survived.

Contact with eastern Europe during the colonization of the regions east of the Elbe and Saale is reflected in loan-words from Polish: *Grenze* (*granica*), *Quark* (*twaróg*), *Kummet* (*chomąt*), *Peitsche* (*bicz*); Czech: *Preiselbeere* (*bruslina*), *Petschaft* (*pečet*), *Pistole* (*pištal*); and Hungarian: *Dolmetscher* (*tolmács*). In more recent times eastern Europe has provided, for example, *Tornister*, *Polka* (Czech *tanistra*, *polka*), *Gulasch* (Hungarian *gulyás* 'cow-herd'), *Grippe*, *Steppe* (Russian *khrip* 'hoarseness', *step*), as well as the international words *Sowjet*, *Bolschewik*, *Komintern*, *Sputnik*. Place-names such as *Berlin*, *Leipzig*, *Dresden*, *Breslau*, *Stettin*[1] are of Slavonic origin.

German contacts with Italy since the Middle Ages have been close and various and account for loan-words in many fields, military and commercial, artistic and scholarly.[2] They begin in the twelfth and thirteenth centuries with *spazieren* (*spaziare*), *Joppe* (*giuppa*), *Zucker* (*zucchero*), continue in the fourteenth and fifteenth with *Golf* (*golfo*), *Kompaß* (*compasso*), *Lack* (*lacca*), *Bank* (*banco*), *Konto* (*conto*), *Melone* (*mellone*), *Kapuze* (*capuccio*), *Matratze* (*materazzo*), and especially since the sixteenth century with *Kanone* (*cannone*), *Arsenal* (*arsenale*), *Granate* (*granata*), *Kavallerie* (*cavalleria*), *Galeere* (*galera*), *Fregatte* (Venetian *fregada*), *Kasse* (*cassa*), *Kredit* (*credito*), *Bilanz* (*bilancio*), *Marzipan* (*marzapane*), *Zitrone* (*citrone*), *Pokal* (*boccale*), and with a few loan translations: *Blumenkohl* (*cavolfiore* cf. *Karfiol* in Austria), *Zwieback* (*biscotto*). In the field of music Italy, as a pioneer in oratorio, opera and other genres, made its most notable contribution to the German vocabulary; a few words, such as *Motette* (*mottetto*), in the fifteenth century were forerunners of a huge influx of terms in the sixteenth and especially the seventeenth:

[1] The names of the last two towns, which are now in Poland, have again been given a Slavonic form: *Wrocław*, *Szczecin*.
[2] Some Italian loan-words have their origin in Arabic and other oriental languages. No attempt is made to distinguish such words here.

A short history of the German language

Kapelle (capella), in the sense of 'orchestra', *Tenor (tenore)*, *Baß
(basso)*, *Oper (opera)*, *Sonate (sonata)*, *Konzert (concerto)*, *Adagio,
Arie (aria)*, *Violoncell (violoncello)*.

But from the late fourteenth to the early seventeenth centuries it
was once again – for the third and last time – Latin which provided
most of the loan-words in German. The Renaissance in Germany,
at least in its literary aspects, was mostly confined to humanist
scholars in the many new universities and schools; their literary
activities were dominated by the academic language, Latin. The
technical vocabulary of academic life – *Akademie, Fakultät, Professor, Doktor, Student, Examen, Gymnasium,* including the names of
school classes, *Prima, Sekunda*, etc. – is still in use today. The various
fields of scholarship are represented by *Philosophie, Logik, Argu-
ment, Definition, Spekulation, Problem, Summe, Nummer, addieren,
subtrahieren, Astronomie, Firmament, Medizin, Medikament, Tinktur,
Podagra, Glosse, Eloquenz, interpretieren.* The older vocabulary of
music was Latin, not Italian: *Terz, Takt, Harmonie, Komponist.*
Printers borrowed many terms: *Initiale, Manuskript, Faksimile,
Kolumne.* Law was especially well represented – contemporaries
complained that lawyers used Latin terms just to mislead laymen! –
*Advokat, Syndikus, Obligation, Prozeß, Delinquent, protestieren,
adoptieren.* To the lawyers we owe the full Latin names of months:
Januarius, Februarius, etc., which replace the traditional names (e.g.
Hornung 'February', *Lenzmonat* 'March', *Brachmonat* 'June', *Heu-
monat* 'July'), and even the older 'Latin' names *Jänner*,[1] *Feber*, etc.
(Of these only *März* survives.) Loan translations were also numerous
and varied: *Wohlwollen (benevolentia), Sittlichkeit (moralitas),
Aberglaube (superstitio), Zeitgenosse (synchronus), Kegelschnitt
(sectio conica), viereckig (quadrangulus), Brennpunkt (punctum
ustionis), Gesichtspunkt (punctum visus).* In many cases loan-words
and loan translations have both survived, though sometimes with
different meanings: *Orthographie, Rechtschreibung; Konsonant, Mit-
laut; Deklination, Beugung; Grammatik, Sprachkunst* (later *Sprachlehre); Chirurg, Wundarzt; liberal, freigebig; Architektur, Baukunst;
Drama, Schauspiel; Zentrum, Mittelpunkt.*

Since the sixteenth century German has taken over loan-words
from many parts of the world,[2] from eastern Europe and Italy, as

[1] *Jänner, Febrer* survive in Austria and in south German and Swiss dialects.
[2] At the same time the standard language, by 'internal borrowing', has drawn
many words from regional dialects (*Föhn, Gletscher, Rucksack* from the Alpine
region, *Eigenbrötler* from Swabia, *Eiland, Fliese, Schnurrbart, Schnaps, barsch,*

78

The German vocabulary: borrowing

we have seen; from Spain (*Infanterie, Armada, Gala*); from Holland (*baggern, bugsieren, Dose, Kai, Küste, Lotterie, Matjeshering, Vlies, Waffel*); and from Scandinavia (*Eider (-ente), Ski, Tang,* even *Erlkönig!*). From outside Europe, Arabic gave *Kattun, Sofa,* Turkish *Kaviar, Joghurt,* Persian *Basar, Karawane,* while American languages account for *Kakao, Mais, Schokolade, Tabak, Tomate, Zigarre, Mokassin, Opossum, Skunk, Wigwam.* From Australia came *Känguruh,* from Africa *Zebra, Schimpanse,* from Japan *Bonze, Kimono, Geisha.* But the most important sources of loan-words in the last four centuries have undoubtedly been French and English.

French loan-words reflect, among other things, the military importance of France in German history (*Armee, Artillerie, Brigade, General, Kaserne, Leutnant, Offizier, Soldat, Truppe*), the repercussions of successive French revolutions (*Revolution, Reaktion, Emigrant, Monarchist, Konstitution, Bourgeois, Sozialismus*), French influences in philosophy, literature, and the arts (*Genie, Humanität, Dekadenz, Milieu, Positivismus, Naturalismus, existentiell, Statue, surrealistisch*). Above all, the prestige of France in domestic and social life becomes clear (*Möbel, Tasse, Perücke, Konversation, Maske, Dame, Mode, Taille, Kavalier, galant, karessieren, Mätresse, Journal, abonnieren*); indeed many words in this field were originally borrowed more for reasons of fashion and snobbery than because of real need (*amüsieren, Revanche, miserabel, simpel, vulgär, Onkel, Tante, Affäre*).

English loan-words do not begin to appear until the middle of the eighteenth century; from then on, however, English influence is strong and continuous.[1] The earliest borrowings are chiefly words drawn from literature (*Ballade, Elfe, Spleen, Humor, sentimental*); but the greatest number are found in the fields of social life (*Klub, Toast, Gentleman, flirten*), food and drink (*Beefsteak, Pudding, Keks, Bowle*), dress (*Frack, Cape, Plaid, Smoking, Pullover, Schal*), politics (*Parlament, Bill, Adresse, Streik, Boykott*), commerce and shipping (*Clearing, Konzern, Scheck, Banknote, Manager, Steward, Pier*),

---

stauen from Low German) and from the specialized vocabulary of professional and other groups (*naseweis, unbändig, vorlaut* from hunting, *Fundgrube, Stichprobe* from mining, *brandmarken, überzeugen* from legal language, *Backfisch, Philister* from students' slang). Learned revival accounts for the re-establishment of once obsolete words like *Minne, Hain, Hort,* and *hehr.*

[1] English has played an important role in transmitting oriental and other non-European words to German: *Punsch, Rum, Polo, Shampoo, Veranda, Pyjama, Dschungel, Jute, Gong, Khaki.*

industry and technology (*Tunnel, Lokomotive, Lift, Koks, Film*), and sport and entertainment (*Sport, Tennis, Match, Start, Rekord, Jockey, Handicap, Camping, Clown*). In the twentieth century, and especially since the First World War, American English[1] has exercised an ever-increasing influence (*Revolver, Trust, Jazz, lynchen, Cocktail, Gangster, Sex-appeal*).

As in earlier periods, the borrowing of words was accompanied by the formation of loan translations in varying degrees of strictness. The following, based on French and English originals, are only a few examples chosen from among many: *folgerichtig* (*conséquent*), *Fortschritt* (*progrès*), *Geschäftsmann* (*homme d'affaires*), *Kehrreim* (*refrain*), *Redensart* (*façon de parler*), *Regenschirm* (*parapluie*), *Staatsbürger* (*citoyen*), *Tagesordnung* (*ordre du jour*), *Unstern* (*désastre*), *Waffenstillstand* (*armistice*); *Blaustrumpf* (*bluestocking*), *Buchmacher* (*bookmaker*), *Dampfer* (*steamer*), *Heilsarmee* (*Salvation Army*), *Jungfernrede* (*maiden speech*), *Leitartikel* (*leading article*), *Thronrede* (*speech from the throne*), *Volkslied* (*popular song*), *Wolkenkratzer* (*skyscraper*).

Some of these loan translations were formed, not for the sake of clarity, but from a desire to purify the language. For the influx of loan-words did not proceed unopposed. At various periods since the Renaissance the use of such words has been condemned and deliberate attempts have been made to replace them by native ones. In the sixteenth century Luther used loan words sparingly, and some of his contemporaries protested vigorously at excessive use of them. But the first sustained attack came in the seventeenth century from the *Sprachgesellschaften*,[2] whose members introduced *Sprachlehre* for *Grammatik*, *Wörterbuch* for *Lexikon*, *Zeitwort* for *Verbum*, *Zahlwort* for *Numerale*, *Briefwechsel* for *Correspondance*, *Mundart* for *Dialekt*, *Trauerspiel* for *Tragödie*, *Verfasser* for *Autor*, and many others, including some whose failure to survive surely needs no explanation: *Zitterweh* for *Fieber*, *Jungfernzwinger* for *Nonnenkloster*, *Leichentopf* for *Urne*!

In the eighteenth century the predominance of France, and, later, the popularity of English culture were hardly favourable to such attempts at purification; by 1800 the number of loan-words was greater than ever. It is true that Klopstock and Lessing, Herder and

---

[1] Germans tend to make a more rigid distinction between British and American English than English speakers do; witness the number of novels translated 'aus dem Amerikanischen'.
[2] See p. 48 f.

The German vocabulary: borrowing

Wieland, Goethe and Schiller used loan-words with some restraint; but it was not until the Napoleonic era that popular hostility to France encouraged opposition to the *Verwelschung* of the language. Leaders in this campaign were certain Romantic writers such as Arndt, Fichte, and Fouqué; but the most important figure was probably J. H. Campe, himself no poet but a masterly coiner of words, to whom we owe *Festland* for *Kontinent*, *Kreislauf* for *Zirkulation*, *Stelldichein* for *Rendezvous*, *Tageblatt* for *Journal*, *betonen* for *akzentuieren* and many other 'translations'.

Since then opposition to the use of foreign words has never entirely ceased. It shows a marked increase in periods of nationalism – for example after 1870, in the First World War or during the Hitler era – and eases off when a more cosmopolitan outlook is in favour, as in the decades after 1945. Meanwhile German continues to increase its resources by borrowing. No doubt this process can sometimes be carried to excessive lengths, as a glance at any illustrated magazine will show; but to condemn it entirely would be foolish as well as futile. The richness and variety of the vocabulary, which is such a notable feature of German, is due in no small measure to the elements which the language has absorbed – and will continue to absorb – from foreign cultures.

FOR FURTHER READING

Friedrich Maurer and Friedrich Stroh (eds.), *Deutsche Wortgeschichte*, 3 vols., 2nd edn., 1959–60 (a composite work covering the whole development of vocabulary from Indo-European to modern German)

Alfred Schirmer, *Deutsche Wortkunde: eine kulturgeschichtliche Betrachtung des deutschen Wortschatzes*, 5th edn. by Walter Mitzka, 1965. (Sammlung Göschen, No. 929)

Werner Betz, *Deutsch und Lateinisch: die Lehnbildungen der althochdeutschen Benediktinerregel*, 1949

Peter F. Ganz, *Der Einfluß des Englischen auf den deutschen Wortschatz 1640–1815*, 1957 (additional material in Philip M. Palmer, *The influence of English on the German vocabulary to 1800*, 1960)

CHAPTER 9

The German vocabulary: change of meaning

The third main way in which the vocabulary develops is by changes in the meaning of words. Here we are not concerned with new words, as in the last two chapters, but with existing words which come to acquire new meanings. This kind of development is very common, for nearly every word has changed its meaning to some extent in the course of its history. It is also extremely varied and elusive, for changes take place continually, and not in the readily observable realm of spoken sound and written symbol, but in the realm of the mind; and they are affected by all the complexities of human psychology and the life of society. All we can do in this chapter is to describe the most common *kinds* of change and indicate some of their more important causes. The categories we use will cover many, perhaps most, cases; but some individual words will still fall outside their scope.

In speaking of the meaning of a word it is useful to distinguish between basic sense and emotive overtones. In the group *die, decease, expire, pass away, pop off*, for example, all the words and phrases have the basic sense of 'cease to live' (though some, of course, have other meanings as well); but each has different overtones. *Decease* is legal and official, *expire* is stiff and literary, *pass away* is mild and spares the feelings, *pop off* is a heartless and comic vulgarism. Both these aspects of meaning, basic sense and emotive overtones, are difficult to define. Some scholars, for instance, hold that a word has no meaning in itself at all, but only acquires one in a specific context. This extreme view is hardly tenable; the word *horse*, for example, when heard in isolation, will evoke roughly the same image in the minds of all English speakers. But the context does indeed play an important part in determining meaning, especially in the case of words with a wide range of senses. It alone can show whether *hot* means 'of a high temperature' or 'strong', as a scent in hunting, or 'fast and rhythmic', as in jazz, or 'difficult to dispose of', as stolen jewels. Emotive overtones are even more dependent on the context; *boy* is emotionally neutral in many contexts, but it acquires a tone of friendly – or perhaps offensive – familiarity when one is addressed as 'old boy'.

How, then, are we to classify the changes of meaning in the German vocabulary? There is no universally recognized and all-embracing scheme, but only a number of traditional categories, of which the following complementary pairs are the most important:

(a) *Extension and restriction of meaning.*[1] Extension of meaning is probably the commonest type of semantic[2] change. *Feder* originally meant 'feather', then also 'quill pen', later still 'pen of any material', and it has also come to mean 'metal spring'. *Schildern* originally referred to the painting of shields – an important occupation in chivalric society; today it means 'depict' regardless of the medium. *Genosse, Gefährte, Geselle* once referred to the sharing of possessions, journeys (cf. *fahren*) and lodgings (cf. *Saal*) respectively; now all mean 'companion', though each has developed new specialized meanings and overtones as well. *Limonade* was once made of lemons; now it means any 'fruit drink' (e.g. *Himbeerlimonade*) while the real lemon drink is *Zitronade* or even *Zitronenlimonade*!

Restriction of meaning is hardly less common than its opposite. *Abendmahl* originally meant 'supper' but now refers only to 'the Lord's Supper', the sacrament of Communion. *Ehe*, from OHG. *ēwa* 'law', is restricted to one kind of law, the marriage contract. *Hochzeit*, once a 'festival' of any sort, now means only a 'wedding'. *Eltern*, 'parents', was originally the comparative of the adjective *alt* and referred to older people in general; similarly *Jünger*, 'disciples', once the comparative of *jung*, meant simply 'younger people'.

Many words, of course, have been both extended and restricted in meaning at different times in their history. *Ehe*, restricted as we have seen, has now acquired the meaning of 'marriage' in all its aspects. *Strahl*, originally an 'arrow', developed the meaning of 'ray of light' and 'jet of water', but has lost its original sense. *Gast*, which originally meant 'stranger', still meant both 'guest' and 'enemy' in early

[1] Ger. *Bedeutungserweiterung, Bedeutungsverengung.*
[2] i.e. 'relating to meaning', from Gk. *sēmaínein* 'to show, signify'.

A short history of the German language

Middle High German; now the latter meaning has gone but new ones have appeared, e.g. *Fahrgast*, 'passenger'.

(b) *Improvement and worsening of meaning.*[1] These categories are less simple than the first pair, for we must always ask: improvement or worsening in what sense? morally? socially? stylistically? or in some other ways? and according to whose scale of values? *Demokratisch*, for example, was a term of abuse in Nazi Germany; *Kirche* will mean something different to the devout Christian and the militant atheist. Nevertheless, if these ambiguities are kept in mind, these categories have some values.

Comparatively few words, it seems, have improved in meaning – a comment, no doubt, on human nature rather than on the German character! *Abendmahl* and *Andacht* (originally 'the direction of the mind to some object', now 'devotion') are restricted to religious contexts. *Lenz* 'spring' and *Odem* 'breath' are confined to high literary style. *Schalk*, once a 'servant', has improved socially; whether it has improved morally is most debatable. *Marschall*, OHG. *marahascalc*, 'horse-servant, groom' rose to mean 'officer in nobleman's household' and now means 'high military officer'. *Pferd* may also be said to have improved; once a 'post-horse, hack', it now covers all kinds of horses, including the noblest.

Much more frequently words have declined in meaning. The medieval titles of nobility *Herr* and *Frau* are now used in all social classes. *Fräulein* implied high social class until the early nineteenth century, as Gretchen's first words to Faust show:

FAUST: Mein schönes Fräulein! Darf ich wagen,
meinen Arm und Geleit Ihr anzutragen?
MARGARETE: Bin weder Fräulein, weder schön.
Kann ungeleitet nach Hause gehn.
(Goethe, *Faust* I, 2605–8).

Knecht, originally 'boy, youth', etc., acquired the meaning of 'servant', even 'serf'. (Its English cognate *knight*, on the other hand, has greatly improved in meaning.) *List* has declined from 'knowledge, wisdom, skill' to 'cunning', while *Gift*, once 'a thing given' (cf. Eng. *gift*), now means 'poison', and *albern*, from OHG. *alawāri* 'completely honest, kindly' now means 'silly, stupid'. Even *ihr*, the foreign pronoun of address in earlier days, is now restricted to

[1] Ger. *Bedeutungsverbesserung, Bedeutungsverschlechterung.*

84

familiar usage; the respectful form is *Sie*.[1] Foreign words, especially French words, have sometimes acquired a pejorative meaning they did not have in their original language: *Pöbel (peuple)* 'mob', *Kumpan* (*compagnon*) 'mate', *Mamsell (mademoiselle)* 'shop-girl, servant'.

(c) *Concrete sense to abstract; abstract sense to concrete.* In its early stages, we may suppose, language was mainly concerned with concrete things and activities; only as thinking became more abstract and man learned to classify specific things in general categories were words adapted to express general ideas, abstract qualities, mental activities and the like. *Fassen* still means 'to put in a container', but it has developed a wide variety of abstract meanings: 'to apprehend, grasp (ideas)', etc. A comparison of *begreifen, ausdrücken, verstehen, unternehmen, unterhalten* with their simple verbs will show the same tendency. *Grille* 'cricket' has also the abstract sense of 'whim, fancy', *Laune*, from Lat. *luna* 'moon', now means 'mood', *Neigung*, like its English equivalent 'inclination', still shows its connection with a sloping surface. *Elend*, once 'foreign country' (OHG. *elilenti*), acquired the meaning first of 'exile', then of 'misery'.

Among the abstract words which have acquired concrete meaning are a number of abstract derivatives in *-ung* and *-schaft* which may also refer to the persons connected with the activity or idea: *Regierung, Bedienung, Dienerschaft, Gesellschaft*. Otherwise only a number of isolated words must be noted: *Uhr*, from Latin *hora* 'hour', means 'clock, watch' – except indeed in phrases like *drei Uhr*; but is this not a contraction of *drei an der Uhr*? *Gespenst* originally meant 'enticement' (OHG. *spanan* 'lure, entice'); now it means 'ghost' – though whether that is concrete is a matter of debate. *Gemach*, originally 'quietness, comfort' is now a somewhat elevated word for 'apartment, chamber'.

These purely descriptive classifications, however, are only a preliminary sorting of evidence;[2] to find what role such changes play in the whole history of the language we must try to discover their

---

[1] See p. 76.
[2] They also represent a valuable discipline for the student of literature, who must be made aware of such changes in meaning in order to gain a full and satisfying understanding of the older literature. This is true not only of the obvious differences between the Middle Ages and today (e.g. MHG. *muot* 'mind, intellect, disposition', etc., modern *Mut* 'courage'), but more particularly of the subtle and, for the foreigner, elusive changes that have taken place since, say, the eighteenth century, when *schlecht* still often meant 'simple, unpretentious' and *bewußtlos* 'unaware' as well as 'unconscious' in the medical sense.

causes. But first, a word about two methods of investigation may not be out of place here.

Words do not exist in isolation, but fall into groups which have been called word-fields (*Wortfelder*) but which might more appropriately be called conceptual fields (*Begriffsfelder*). These are groups of closely associated ideas and the words that express them, e.g. *List, Kunst, Weisheit, Wissenschaft, Gelehrsamkeit, Bildung* in the field of the intellect[1] or the various words for 'female human being' (*Frau, Weib, Dame, Fräulein, Jungfrau, Mädchen, Magd,* etc.). Changes of meaning within such a group do not take place in isolation, but rather the words affect each other in extremely complex ways. Conceptual fields must remain outside the scope of this book, but even a brief reference will serve to emphasize the fact that a language is a coherent structure, in vocabulary as well as in its formal aspects, and to remind the reader that the word-histories in this chapter are no more than mere hints at a much more complex development.[2]

The second technique starts from the fact that meaning is essentially the relationship between the physical word and the idea it conveys, between sound and sense. We may therefore begin with the word and ask how its sense changes, what new meanings it acquires, what older meanings are lost. This has been the normal approach to semantic problems in the nineteenth and early twentieth centuries. But we may also begin with the sense and ask what different words have been used to express it and why one word has displaced another. This approach is very ancient,[3] but has only recently found favour again. The two approaches are complementary and can both be used as need arises.

In looking for the causes of semantic change we need to take account first of all of a number of psychological mechanisms which seem to be continually at work in the formation and development of vocabulary. The most important of these are represented by metaphor and metonymy and to a lesser extent by popular etymology.

---

[1] This was the subject of a famous investigation by Professor Jost Trier of Münster, to whom research into word-fields owes a great debt.

[2] Readers will find much interest and enjoyment in looking up the fuller histories of words mentioned here in dictionaries such as Grimm, Trübner, *Duden, Etymologie,* and Kluge-Mitzka (full titles in bibliography, p. 159).

[3] It is also the basis of such dictionaries as Roget's *Thesaurus,* first published in 1852, in which the words of English are arranged according to the ideas they express. Wehrle-Eggers *Deutscher Wortschatz* does the same for the German language.

Metaphor depends on the ability of the human mind to detect similarities between ideas or things which at first sight seem remote. The modern meanings of *Strahl*, already mentioned, depend on the similarity of shape and direction between arrows, rays, and jets. *Begreifen* involves similarity of action, seizing with the hands and seizing with the mind. *Linse* 'lentil' develops the sense of 'lens' because of similarity of shape. *Strom* 'current' is used of electricity on the assumption that electricity flows through the wires. *Werben*, originally 'to turn round', develops the sense 'to woo', possibly because of the behaviour of birds and animals in courtship; a further metaphor leads to the sense 'to win supporters', e.g. in politics or by advertising. The original meaning of *schön* 'pleasing to the sight', *süß* 'pleasing to the taste' and *hell* 'clear' (of sound) have been generalized to apply in the field of other physical senses than the original ones: 'beautiful', 'sweet', 'bright'. Sometimes the metaphor involves a whole phrase. *Einen Bock schießen* 'commit a blunder' is a metaphor drawn from hunting; *jemand übertrumpfen* 'outwit, outdo someone' comes from card-playing. These phrases account for the sense of *Bock* as 'blunder' and of *Trumpf* as 'advantage'.

Metonymy depends not on similarity but on some other kind of close connection between the old sense and the new.[1] Here belong the many words derived from personal and place names, names of inventors and discoverers, places of origin of commercial products, and the like; a simple list of such words may tempt the reader to discover their origins for himself: *Ampère, Biedermeier, boykottieren, Fayence, fuggern, Grobian, Heller, Kannegießer, Kognak, makadamisieren, Musselin, Perser, Taler, verballhornen, Volt*. It may indeed be that all names were originally proper names, i.e. labels of particular things, and became generalized as primitive man learned to think in more general categories. Here, too, belong *Bursche*, once 'a students' hostel', now a name for the student himself; *Universität*, originally the 'company of students and teachers', now extended to the building as well; *Chor* 'choir of clergy in church', then 'group of singers', now also 'place in church where clergy and singers stand'. Further examples, involving abstract qualities or capacities and the people associated with them, are *Wache, Zunft, Regierung, Herrschaft, Nachbarschaft*. A specially common type of metonymy is the so-called *pars pro toto*, where part of something stands for the whole: *Segel*

---

[1] For a discussion of this wider use of the term *metonymy* see S. Ullmann, *Semantics*, 1962.

for *Schiff*, *Dach* for *Haus*, *Seele* or *Kopf* for *Person*, *Rotkehlchen*,[1] now the normal name of the red-breasted bird, *Bulle*, where the 'leaden seal' on the document has become the name of the papal edict; also, in a more symbolical sense, *Krone* for the monarchy and *Altar* for the Church.

Metaphor and metonymy are extremely common in German as in English. Both devices arise from a desire to make expression more vivid and forceful, and it is difficult to imagine language functioning adequately without them. Popular etymology is much less extensive and inevitable in its functioning, but it too has a considerable effect on the language. It consists of a historically incorrect association between a word whose etymology has become obscure and a more familiar word. Though it leads more often to changes in the form of the word, the meaning, or at least the emotive overtones, are often affected as well. OHG. *hagustalt* meant the owner of a *hag*, a small plot of ground too small to support a family; hence the further meaning 'bachelor'. The second element was then associated with *stolz*; hence the modern form *Hagestolz* 'bachelor', but with the suggestion of one who is proud of his bachelorhood, a 'gay bachelor'. OHG. *helfantbein* 'ivory' (literally 'elephant bone') was associated with *Elfe*; the modern form *Elfenbein*, though still meaning 'ivory', suggests something of the fairy world. French *valise* appears in Middle High German as *velīs* or *velīsen*. This was remodelled as *Felleisen* by association with *Fell* and *Eisen*, which seems to suggest that a 'portmanteau' is something made of hide and iron.

Metaphor, metonymy, and popular etymology, however, are not the causes of semantic change but rather represent common ways in which changes are brought about. The real causes of change must be sought elsewhere. We may begin with a few special cases where the state of the language itself predisposes to change.

There seems to be a tendency in language to avoid exact synonyms. When these occur some sort of differentiation takes place. Compared with *Pferd*, *Adler*, *Frühling*, *Atem*, *Träne*, the near-synonyms *Roß*, *Aar*, *Lenz*, *Odem*, *Zähre* sound formal, old-fashioned, and 'poetical'; even *Junge* and *Knabe* show a similar difference. Or the synonyms develop differences of meaning. *Haupt*, a near-synonym of *Kopf*, is more formal and poetical; but it has also acquired transferred meanings, cf. *Hauptstadt*, *Oberhaupt*. In the eighteenth century *Anmerkung* meant '(spoken) comment' and *Be-*

---

[1] For compounds like *Rotkehlchen* see pp. 61–2 (possessive compounds).

merkung 'observation'; *Bemerkung* has now acquired the meaning of 'comment, remark', while *Anmerkung* means a written 'note' in scholarly writing. The shift may be partly due to the presence of *Beobachtung* 'observation', i.e. in one of the earlier senses of *Bemerkung*. In Middle High German *schon* and *fast* were the adverbs corresponding to the adjectives *schön* and *fest*. Later the formal distinctions between adjectives and adverbs disappeared; with few exceptions, adjectives can now be used as adverbs. *Schon* and *fast* have survived only because of (somewhat complicated) shifts in meaning. *Drücken* and *drucken* represent a rather different situation. They were the Middle German and Upper German forms of a single verb meaning 'to press'. *Drucken* acquired the specialized meaning 'to print', because the principal early printing centres were in Southern Germany.

The opposite situation, in which a single word develops a wide range of meaning, often arises. In most cases the context alone is enough to indicate the appropriate meaning. In Vienna *Ananas* denotes a large cultivated strawberry (shortened form of *Ananaserdbeere*); but it still retains its more usual meaning of 'pineapple'; and even in the strawberry season *Ananaskompott* would hardly be made from strawberries. But occasionally it is convenient to make a formal distinction. In Old High German *ander* meant both 'other' and 'second'; the latter meaning was transferred to *zweit*, an analogical form which completed the pattern *erst . . . dritt, viert*, etc. In words which have developed alternative plural forms or genders, these were used to distinguish meanings: *Länder, Lande; Worte, Wörter; Männer, Mannen, Mann; Orte, Örter; die See, der See*.

Loan-words have at first no organic connection with the rest of the language and are open to misinterpretation. *Stiefel* comes ultimately from *aestivale*, 'a high summer boot' (Lat. *aestas* 'summer'); but speakers who knew no Latin did not see the connection with summer and used the word for other kinds of boot. In *Plaid* the emphasis is on the tartan pattern and the function as a travelling-rug; the fact that it originally designated the outer wrap in a Highlander's dress is forgotten. *Zoll*, from Latin *telōneum* 'customs house' is now the 'customs-money' – but this may rather be an example of metonymy.

But the real causes of semantic change lie, as so often in language, outside language itself. The desire to soften the effect of a statement by euphemism, i.e. by the use of a milder word in place of the harsh literal term, goes back in part to primitive taboos; 'speak of the devil and he'll appear' reflects the same ancient fear. This is probably why *bear* (Ger. *Bär*) is called, literally, 'the brown one' (contrast Lat. *ursus*, Fr. *ours*) and why names for the right and left hands in many languages imply the 'skilful or powerful' member and the 'sinister, weak, awkward' member respectively. Other euphemisms arise from a desire to spare the hearer's feelings or to avoid mentioning directly – and therefore facing – disagreeable subjects. *Entschlafen* and *entschlummern* mean 'to die, pass away'; *Abort, Nachtstuhl, verschwinden, hinausgehen* need no comment in a country where one goes to the 'toilet' to 'wash one's hands'.

The opposite tendency to use a cruder or more violent term than is strictly necessary has led to the use of *Rindvieh, Schwein, Lump* as terms of personal abuse, of *die großen Kanonen* or *das große Gemüse* to express disrespect or envious respect, or of *Schelm, Kerl, Lausbub* as terms of endearment. Excessive and indiscriminate use of words with strong emotive overtones soon leads to their weakening; *schrecklich, furchtbar, ungeheuer, fabelhaft, kolossal, phantastisch, prima, erstklassig* are hardly more vivid than 'good' or 'bad'; and is there anything left in the first elements of *Pfundskerl, Mordshunger, Heidenangst,* or *blutjung* except a slangy flavour? Most usage of this kind is colloquial and changes rapidly according to fashion; but at least one such weakened word has remained in the standard language: *sehr*, once meaning 'painfully' (cf. Eng. *sore*) and now the colourless adverb for 'very'.

Strong emotion can contribute to other kinds of semantic change. A word involved in heated controversy often acquires overtones which remain long after the controversy is over. *Pfaffe* had at first no pejorative meaning. But in medieval anti-clerical writings it declined in favour of *Pfarrer* and *Priester*; and the Reformation, with its attacks on clerical shortcomings, completed the process. Its present meaning, 'corrupt or bigoted priest', is no doubt reinforced by its hissing, spitting sound. Words like *Parteigenosse, Rassentheorie, Führerprinzip*, once prominent in National Socialist ideology, are likely to provoke strong resentment for some time to come. *Demokratie*, on the other hand, has been rescued from its use by the Nazis as a sneering term of abuse.[1]

[1] Some scholars have drawn attention to what they term *Sprachlenkung*, a deliberate manipulation of the meaning of words by public authorities for propaganda purposes. *Der große Duden: Rechtschreibung*, published at Leipzig in 1959,

The German vocabulary: change of meaning

In quite general terms, the main cause of semantic changes is the process of civilization. Many of the examples in this chapter, though used here in other contexts, reflect changes in ideas, in science and technology and in social institutions. We add a few more examples from different periods of German history.

The introduction of Christianity with its many new ideas and practices led to the appearance of loan-words and loan translations in abundance.[1] Other words, without changing their form, acquired new meanings under the influence of foreign terms. *Heiland, Beichte, Buße, Hölle* have already been mentioned. *Andacht*, on the other hand, owes its specialized meaning to Cistercians in the twelfth century, while *fromm* (originally 'useful', cf. *frommen* 'to be of use') and *Abendmahl* develop their modern meanings only with the Reformation.

Courtly culture produced many semantic changes, including many instances of borrowed meaning. Most of the technical terms in the chivalric moral code were influenced by French or Latin models. Two examples must suffice here. On the level of material culture we have the MHG. word *kemenate*, from Lat. (*camera*) *caminata*, 'room with a fireplace'; *Kamin* 'fireplace', from Lat. *camina*, still survives. In the rough living conditions of the medieval castle the *kemenate* was allotted to the ladies, so the word acquired the meaning of 'women's quarters'. (In later middle-class society the heated room was the *Stube*, a word meaning first a 'stove' (its English cognate), then the bathroom heated by a stove, later the heated living-room and finally other rooms in the house; cf. *Schlafstube, die gute Stube.*) Perhaps the most characteristic word in this period, at any rate in courtly literature, is *minne*. In Old High German *minna* had designated – among other things – love, in all its aspects, divine and human. From its continual use in connection with the philosophy

gives: '*Kapital*: Wert, der seinem Besitzer, dem Kapitalisten, durch Ausbeutung von Lohnarbeitern Mehrwert bringt'; '*liberal*, . . . *im Kapitalismus mißbraucht im Sinne von* ungehemmte Freiheit für die wirtschaftliche Betätigung des bürgerlichen Individuums gewährend'; '*Aktivist*, anerkannter Neuerer im Arbeitsprozeß'; '*Kollektiv*, Arbeits-, Produktionsgemeinschaft zur Erreichung gemeinsamer Ziele'; '*Sozialismus*, eine auf der Grundlage der politischen Herrschaft der Arbeiterklasse beruhende Gesellschaftsordnung, in der die Produktionsmittel in gesellschaftliches Eigentum übergeführt sind und die Ausbeutung des Menschen durch den Menschen beseitigt ist'. Is all this any more than an attempt to reflect accepted (East German) usage? Or has it any effect as propaganda? At all events some words in East Germany are changing their meaning, apparently with official approval.

[1] See p. 73ff.

A short history of the German language

and practice of courtly love it acquired an ever more specialized meaning until it was finally ousted by *Liebe*, which had meant 'happiness, joy', then 'affection'. As courtly culture declined, stress was laid on the illicit aspect of courtly love; *minne* thus acquired a pejorative meaning and by the sixteenth century it was regarded as obscene. It was revived as a technical term by eighteenth-century poets and scholars.

In the modern world science and technology play an important role. Simple technological advances of an older period are reflected in the development of *Feder, Glas, Papier, Tisch, Horn, Rohr, Diele, Kork*, and many other words. In modern times the sciences have relied greatly for their terminology on an international vocabulary with many Latin and Greek roots – examples are too well known to need mention – while technology has been more inclined to form new words with native elements or to adapt existing words to new meanings. Our few examples come from a single branch of technology close to ordinary life, broadcasting: *Radio, Mikrophon, Antenne* are loan-words, *Kurzwelle, Lautsprecher, Fernsehen* are loan translations, *Sender* and *Empfänger* show borrowing of meaning, *Kurzwellensender, Sportsendung, Rundfunkgerät, Radioansager* are only a few of many compounds . . . From science and technology, from politics and economics, from sport and entertainment, and from many other sources new words and new meanings come every year to enrich the language. It is hardly likely – nor indeed to be wished – that such changes and additions will stop or decrease.

FOR FURTHER READING

Stephen Ullmann, *Semantics: an introduction to the science of meaning*, 1962

Helmut A. Hatzfeld, *Leitfaden der vergleichenden Bedeutungslehre: eine Zusammenstellung charakteristischen semasiologischen Beispielmaterials aus den bekanntesten Sprachen*, 2nd edn., 1928

Hans Sperber, *Einführung in die Bedeutungslehre*, 3rd edn., 1965

Franz Dornseiff, *Bezeichnungswandel unseres Wortschatzes: Ein Blick in das Seelenleben des Sprechenden*. Siebente neubearbeitete Auflage von Albert Waag, 'Bedeutungsentwicklung unseres Wortschatzes, ein Blick in das Seelenleben der Wörter', 1966

Part III

CHAPTER 10

Sound changes from Indo-European to Germanic

In this survey of the development of German sounds prominence is given to a description of the sound changes themselves. Little is said about causes, which in any case are often very obscure. The historical and social context in which the changes take place have already been described in Chapters 3, 5, and 6, and need not be repeated here.

A. VOWEL CHANGES

The Indo-European vowel system has been described on page 9. The following changes (1–9) occurred in the development of Primitive Germanic from Indo-European and are reflected in all the Germanic languages:[1]

(1) IE. *o* > Gmc. *a*:

    L. *octo*   OHG. *ahto*
    L. *hostis*   OHG. *gast*

(2) IE. *ə* > Gmc. *a*:

    IE. **pətēr*   (L. *pater*)   OHG. *fater*

(3) IE. *ā* > Gmc. *ō* (contrast with (1) above):

    L. *māter*   OE. *mōdor*   (OHG. *muoter*)
    L. *fāgus*   OE. *bōc*   (OHG. *buohha*)

---

[1] IE. is represented chiefly by Latin, but occasionally by Greek or even Sanskrit. Germanic examples are taken from OHG. where possible; but where Gothic, Old English, or Old Norse is used for greater clarity, the OHG. form is sometimes added in brackets. Good examples of many of the changes described in this and the next chapter may be found among the strong verbs. But since the reader may wish to test his knowledge of sound changes on the strong verbs in Appendix I, these examples are rarely used in the text.

IE. $\bar{e}$ was probably an open sound. It is noted as $\bar{æ}$ in Gmc., or better still as $\bar{e}^1$ to distinguish it from the closed sound $\bar{e}^2$ (see (4) below). But this is a spelling convention and not a sound change.

(4) IE. $\bar{e}i >$ Gmc. $\bar{e}^2$:

    Gk. *ekei* 'there' OHG. *hēr* (later *hier*, etc.)

This explanation of the origin of Gmc. $\bar{e}^2$ is uncertain. Examples are rare and doubtful.

(5) IE. *ei* > Gmc. $\bar{i}$:

Gk. *steichō* 'I go'	OHG. *stīgan*
Old Lat. *deico* (Classical Lat. *dīco*)	OHG. *zīhan* 'accuse'

Otherwise long diphthongs develop in the same way as the corresponding short ones.

(6) IE. *oi* > Gmc. *ai* (compare (1) above):

    Gk. *oide* 'he knows' Goth. *wait* (OHG. *weiz*)[1]

(7) IE. *ou* > Gmc. *au* (compare (1) above):

    IE. **roudhos* (L. *rūfus*) Goth. *raups* (OHG. *rōt*)

(8) The syllabic consonants *l̥, r̥, m̥, n̥* develop a vowel *u: ul, ur*, etc.:

IE. **wl̥kʷós* (L. *lupus*)	Goth. *wulfs*	(OHG. *wolf*)
IE. **pr̥k-* (L. *porca* 'ridge between furrows')		OE. OHG. *furh*
IE. **k̂m̥tóm* L. (*centum*)	Goth. *hund*	OHG. *hunt*
IE. **dn̥t-* 'tooth'	Goth. *tunþus*	(OHG. *zand*)

(9) When Gmc. *a, i, u* come before a nasal plus a velar fricative (ŋx), the nasal is dropped and the vowel lengthened (compensatory lengthening):

    L. *pango* 'I fasten', Gmc. **faŋxanan* OHG. *fāhan*
        cf. OHG. *bringan, brāhta* (< **braŋxta*)
            dunken, dūhta

---

[1] *z* in OHG. and MHG. represents a sharp s-sound made well forward against the upper teeth. It arises from Gmc. *t* (see p. 112, point (17), and is distinguished from *s*, a sound produced farther back in the mouth, until the thirteenth century (see p. 116, point (25)).

As the nasal consonant was dropped, the vowel was probably nasalized and later denasalized. This may explain why OE. has *ō* and not *ā* here:

$$*braŋxta > *brãxta > \text{OE. } brōhte$$

In Old English and Low German a vowel followed by a nasal and *f, s,* or *þ* was lengthened and the nasal was dropped: compare OHG. *gans, fimf, ander* with OE. *gōs, fīf, ōðer* (with the same OE. variant *ō* as in *brōhte*). This change is not found in High German or elsewhere in Germanic; and the connection between it and the change in point (9) is not entirely clear.

The next changes (10–14) are not found in Gothic,[1] and probably occurred after the separation of the East Germanic tribes:

(10) $ē^1$ ($ǣ$) $> ā$:

    Goth. *jēr*   OHG. *jār*

    Goth. *ētum* (L. *ēdimus*)   OHG. *āȝum*

(11) *e* before nasal plus other consonant $> i$:

    L. *ventus*   OHG. *wint*

    L. *offendix* 'knot, band'   OHG. *bintan*

(12) *e* before *i, j,* or *u* in next syllable $> i$:

    L. *medius*   OHG. *mitti*

    OHG. *berg*   OHG. *gibirgi*

    IE. **sedhus* (Gk. *ethos* 'custom')   OHG. *situ*

The change caused by *u* is less widespread than that caused by *i* or *j*. It seems to be most fully effective in High German, though other North and West Germanic dialects show it to some extent.[2]

(13) *i* before *a, e, o* in next syllable $> e$ (but there are many exceptions):

    L. *vices*   OHG. *wehsal*

    L. *nīdus* (IE. **nizdos*)   OHG. *nest*

                                 (< Gmc. **nestaz*)

---

[1] The fluctuation between *e* and *i, o* and *u* shown in points (11) to (14) is also found in Gothic; but the conditions in which it occurs are quite different.

[2] The terms 'North Germanic' and 'West Germanic' are not intended to imply the existence, at any stage, of 'North Germanic' or 'West Germanic' as unified dialects; cf. the discussion on pp. 23 and 24. They merely refer, in a brief and convenient way, to common features in the North Germanic or West Germanic languages.

(14)   *u* before *a, e, o* in next syllables > *o*:

L. *jugum*	OHG. *joh*
	(< Gmc. **jukan*)
OHG. *wir hulfum*	OHG. *giholfan*

This change restores *o* to the (North and West) Germanic vowel system; cf. point (1) above. It is prevented when *u* is followed by a nasal plus other consonant (cf. change (11) above):

OE. *tunge*	OHG. *zunga*

contrast OHG. *giholfan* and *gibuntan*.

The changes in (13) and (14) are often referred to as *fracture* (*Brechung*).

B. ABLAUT

One further feature of the Germanic vowel system has its origin, not in changes from Indo-European to Germanic, but in changes far back in the Indo-European period itself. (Because of this the points in this section are not numbered consecutively with those in sections A and C.) When we speak of the Indo-European sound system we usually mean only the latest form of that system as it existed before the Indo-European community broke up; for that is all we can reconstruct by comparative methods. But such groups of words as Eng. *sing, sang, sung*, German *helfen, half, geholfen*, or Latin *capio, cēpi* enable us to go back much further and see, however dimly, one feature of Indo-European as it develops. *Helfen, half*, and *geholfen*, it is safe to assume, came from a single root. Yet even by eliminating all the sound changes that have taken place between Indo-European and German we cannot reduce them to a single form. The vowels remain different (IE. **kelbonom, *kolba, *kḷbonos*). They show, in fact, the phenomenon which Jakob Grimm called *Ablaut* (English: 'vowel gradation' or simply 'ablaut').

The Indo-European accent, it will be remembered,[1] was movable, and both musical and dynamic accent played an important part in it. Now when a vowel of a certain length and quality loses its accent or is accented differently it tends to change in quality or quantity or both, or to disappear entirely. This well known process accounts for

[1] See p. 10.

ablaut, though details are not always clear and in any case are too complex to treat fully here.

Ablaut is of two kinds, qualitative, where the basic vowel changes in quality (e.g. *e* becomes *o*), and quantitative, where the basic vowel is lengthened or shortened or disappears (e.g. short *e* becomes long *e* or *ə* or disappears entirely). By combining these two kinds we arrive at an ablaut series, i.e. the different possible variants of a basic vowel. There are at least six ablaut series in Indo-European; but the most important one for Germanic is *e* : *o* : *ē* : *ō* : *ə* : – (where – represents the absence of any vowel). Here *e* and *o* are called the normal grade, *ē* and *ō* the lengthened grade, *ə* the reduced grade, and – the zero grade. The IE. root **sed-* in its various forms develops as follows (only Latin and Germanic forms are noted):

*sed-: L. *sed-ēre* 'to sit'
        Gmc. **set-*: ON. *setr* 'seat'
                *set-jan: Goth. *sitan*, OE. *sittian*, OHG. *sizzen*
*sod-: Gmc. **sat-*: Goth. *sat*, OE. *sæt*, OHG. *saȝ*.
                *sat-jan: Goth. *satjan*, OE. *settan*, OHG. *sezzen*
*sēd-: L. *sēdi* 'I have sat', *sēdes* 'seat'
        Gmc. **sē^{1}t-*: Goth. *sētum*, OE. *sǣton*, OHG. *sāȝun*
*sōd-: Gmc. **sōt-*: OE. *sōt* 'soot' (i.e. something which has settled)
*sd- > **zd-*: IE. **ni-zd-os*: L. *nīdus*
                         Gmc. **nestaz*: OE. OHG. *nest*

In Germanic, ablaut is most fully represented in the forms of the strong verb.[1] But it may also be seen, though less systematically, in other places, for example in the suffixes of comparative and superlative adjectives in Old High German[2] and in groups of etymologically related words, e.g. *loben, erlauben, Gelübde; fliegen, Flügel; sitzen, seßhaft, Sattel*. Sometimes such groups are hardly recognizable at first sight, especially when the original basic element was disyllabic; IE. **genē-*, for example, is the origin, not only of L. *genus*, Eng. *kin*, OHG. *kunni*, but also of L. *natus*. Similarly, Eng. *wolf*, Ger. *Wolf*, are in ablaut relationship to L. *lupus*.

C. CONSONANT CHANGES

(15) The First or Germanic Sound-Shift is the most important of all the sound-changes which distinguish Germanic from other branches

---

[1] See p. 130.   [2] See p. 126.

of Indo-European. Its effects are widespread in all Germanic languages for it involved all the Indo-European plosive consonants. It was probably complete by about 500 B.C., certainly before the first loan-words were borrowed from Latin, for these are unaffected by it. Its causes are very uncertain despite many and varied theories; the effect of the speech habits of a pre-Indo-European population – the so-called substratum theory outlined in Chapter 3[1] – is accepted by many scholars, but not by all. The four phases of the sound shift are as follows (the order given is probably, though by no means certainly, the order in which they occurred):

$$
\begin{array}{llll}
\text{I} & \text{IE.} & p, t, k, k^w & > \text{Gmc. } f, \text{þ}, x, xw \\
\text{II} & & ph, th, kh, kh^w & > \quad\quad f, \text{þ}, x, xw \\
\text{III} & & bh, dh, gh, gh^w & > \quad\quad b, d, g, gw \\
\text{IV} & & b, d, g, g^w & > \quad\quad p, t, k, kw \\
\end{array}
$$

x represents the unvoiced fricative heard in Ger. *ach*. *b̑*, *d̑*, *g̑* represent voiced fricatives, bilabial, dental, and palatal (or velar) respectively.

Note: (a) Very early x was reduced to h initially and between vowels.
(b) Very early $b̑ > b$ initially and after m, $d̑ > d$ initially and after n, $g̑ > g$ only after $ŋ$.

I	$p > f$	L. *pecus*	OHG. *fihu*	
		L. *nepos*	OHG. *nefo*	
	$t > þ$	L. *trēs*	OE. *þrī*	(OHG. *drī*)
		L. *frāter*	Goth. *brōþar*	(OHG. *bruoder*)
	$k > x$	L. *collum*	OHG. *hals*	
		L. *dūcō*	Goth. *tiuhan*	(OHG. *ziohan*)
	$k^w > xw$	L. *quod*	OHG. *hwaz̑ (waz̑)*	

II	$ph > f$	Gk. *sphallein* 'cause to fall'	OHG. *fallan*	
	$th > þ$	Gk. *askēthēs* 'unharmed'	Goth. *skaþjan* 'injure'	(OHG. *scadēn*)
	$kh > x$	Gk. *achnē* 'chaff'	Goth. *ahana* 'chaff'	
	$kh^w > xw$	examples uncertain.		

[1] See p. 17 f.
100

III	$bh > b$	IE. *bher-	OHG. beran	
		(L. fero)		
		*gombh-	OHG. kamb	
		(Gk. gomphos		
		'molar tooth')		
	$dh > d$	IE. *dhe-	OE. dōn 'do'	(OHG. tuon)
		(L. facere)		
		*widhewa	Goth. widuwō	(OHG.
		(L. vidua)	$(d = \eth)$	wituwa)
	$gh > g$	IE. *ghostis	OHG. gast	
		(L. hostis)		
		*angh-	OHG. angi, engi	
		(L. ang-ustus)		
	$gh^w > gw$	IE. *songh^wos	Goth. saggws	(OHG. sang)
			$(gg = ng)$	

IV	$b > p$	Gk. baitē	Goth. paida	(OHG. pfeit)
		'goat-skin coat'		
		L. turba 'crowd'	OE. þorp	(OHG. dorf)
	$d > t$	L. duo	OE. twā	(OHG. zwā)
		L. edo	OE. etan	(OHG.
				ezzan)
	$g > k$	L. genu	OE. cnēo	OHG. kniu
		L. ego	OE. ic	(OHG. ih)
	$g^w > kw$	IE. *g^wem-	OHG. queman	
		(L. venio)		

Exceptions to this general scheme:

(a) sp, st, sk remain unshifted in Germanic:

L. spuere	OHG. spīwan
L. stāre	OHG. stēn
L. est	OHG. ist
L. piscis	OHG. fisk

(b) pt, kt are only partially shifted to ft, xt:

L. captus	OHG. haft 'fettered,
	imprisoned'
L. nox, noctem	OHG. naht

(c) *tt > ss*

> OE. *witan*   OE. *wisse* (past tense; < IE. **witto-* < **wid-to-*)
>
> (cf. OHG. *wiʒʒan, wissa*)[1]

(16) *Verner's Law* accounts for a number of sound changes which were once thought to be anomalies in the working of the first sound-shift. A comparison of the groups L. *frater*, Goth. *brōþar* (OHG. *bruoder*) and L. *pater*, Goth. *fadar* (pronounced *fadar*; OHG. *fater*) show that IE. *t* is treated differently in the two groups in Germanic. The first change, *t > þ*, is in accordance with the first sound-shift; the second, *t > d*, is not. (The OHG. forms are the result of later changes.) The Danish scholar Karl Verner found that these differences had to do with the fact that the Indo-European accent was movable. His explanation may be stated as follows:

The medial and final voiceless fricatives *f, þ, x* (which arose from *p, t, k*) and *s* were regularly voiced to *b, d, g, z*, except when the vowel immediately preceding them carried the main word accent or when they were accompanied by other voiceless consonants. We may note (*a*) that initial consonants and the groups *sp, st, sk, ss, ft, fs, xt, xs* are not affected; (*b*) that the *b, d, g*, thus formed develop exactly like the *b, d, g*, from IE. *bh, dh, gh*; (*c*) that the Germanic accent became fixed on the root syllable (i.e. usually the first syllable) of the word at some time after these changes had taken place.

In *Vater* the accent originally fell on the second syllable, cf. Gk. *patér*; the word will have developed as follows:

IE. *pətér, Gmc. **faþér, fadér, fáder*: Gothic *fadar* (OHG. *fater* by a further shift).

All this leads, in words from the same root (e.g. parts of verbs, etymologically related words) to a fluctuation – called traditionally, though somewhat misleadingly, 'grammatical change' – between Gmc. *f/b, þ/d, x/g* (with *ŋx/ŋg, xw/gw*), *s/z*. Examples will be given later when we see how these sounds develop in High German.[2]

The next four changes (17–20) are not found in Gothic. Points (17) and (18) affect both North and West Germanic:

(17) *z > r*. In West Germanic languages this *r* is dropped when final, except in a few High German monosyllabic pronouns:

---

[1] These forms, OHG. *wiʒʒan*, past indic. *wissa*, survive in MHG. *wiʒʒen ,wisse* (or *wesse*). The alternative forms of the past tense, MHG. *wiste, weste*, are formed by analogy with ordinary weak verbs (see p. 131). The standard form is now *wußte*.

[2] See p. 114.

	Goth. *maiza*	ON. *meiri*		OHG. *mēro*	
Gmc. **dagaz*:	Goth. *dags*	ON. *dagr*		OHG. *tag*	
	Goth. *mis*	ON. *mér*	OE. *mē*	OHG. *mir*	
	Goth. *weis*	ON. *vér*	OE. *wē*	OHG. *wir*	
	Goth. *þus*	ON. *þér*	OE. *ðē*	OHG. *dir*	
	Goth. *jūs*	ON. *ér*	OE. *gē*	OHG. *ir*	
	Goth. *is*	ON. [*hann*]	OE. *hē*	OHG. *er*	

(18) *þl- > fl-:*

Goth. *þliuhan*　　　　　　　OHG. *fliohan*

Points (19) and (20) are found only in West Germanic.

(19) *đ > d* in all positions:

Goth. *fadar*　　ON. *faðir*　　OE. *fæder*　　(OHG. *fater*)

(20) *West Germanic doubling* of consonants is the most notable difference between the West Germanic languages and the rest of Germanic. There were already a few double consonants in Germanic, mostly produced by assimilation:

IE. **pl̥nós* (L. *plēnus*): Goth. *fulls*　OHG. *fol*
　　　　　　　　　　　　　　　　(inflected *follēr*)
IE. **bhugno-*:　　　　　　OE. *bucca*　OHG. *boc, bockes*

In West Germanic every single consonant (except *r*), when followed by *j* and to a lesser extent by *r, l, w*, was doubled:

	Goth. *satjan*	OE. *settan*	(OHG. *sezzen*)
	Goth. *wilja*	OE. *willa*	OHG. *willio, willo*
	Goth. *sibja*	OE. *sibb*	(OHG. *sippea, sippa*)
but:	Goth. *nasjan*	OE. *nerian*	OHG. *nerian, nerien*
	Goth. *akrs*	(OE. *æcer*)	OHG. *ackar*
	ON. *apall, epli*[1]	OE. *æppel*	(OHG. *apful*)
	Goth. *naqaþs*	(OE. *nacod*)	OHG. *nackot*
	(*q = kw*)		

FOR FURTHER READING

Hans Krahe, *Indogermanische Sprachwissenschaft, I: Einleitung und Lautlehre*, 3rd edn., 1958 (Sammlung Göschen No. 59)

Hans Krahe, *Germanische Sprachwissenschaft, I: Einleitung und Lautlehre*, 3rd edn., 1956 (Sammlung Göschen No. 238)

Arthur Kirk, *An introduction to the historical study of New High German*, 1923

[1] 'apple' does not appear in Biblical Gothic (*Genesis* has not survived!). *Apel* is the form in sixteenth-century Crimean Gothic.

103

CHAPTER 11

Sound changes in German

Old High German literature begins about A.D. 770, when the first extant German documents appear.[1] But most of the linguistic features characteristic of the Old High German dialects had begun to develop before then – some as early as the fifth century, it is thought – and many had already reached completion before the first documents were written. We shall make no distinction between the pre-documentary and documentary stages.

In the Old High German period there was no standard language but only a number of literary dialects which differed markedly from each other.[2] A complete study of Old High German sounds and forms would have to take such dialectal variants into account. But here we shall only occasionally mention dialectal differences and shall follow tradition by quoting Old High German words in their East Franconian form. Similarly in the Middle High German period we shall concentrate on the literary language[3] and take no account of dialects, though these, of course, continued to flourish.

The transition to modern times presents another difficulty. The New High German standard language did not develop directly from the Middle High German literary language but rose anew from regional dialects in the late Middle Ages.[4] To compare the two standard languages directly, therefore, is to oversimplify a very complicated historical process. But provided this is kept in mind when we read such comparisons as MHG. *swern*, NHG. *schwören*, there is perhaps no harm in following tradition here again. Certainly we cannot take account of all dialectal variants, not even those which have found their way into the standard language.

[1] See p. 31.
[2] See p. 32 f.
[3] See p. 34 f.
[4] See p. 35 f.

Sound changes in German

A. VOWEL CHANGES

The following six changes are characteristic of Old High German:

(1) Gmc. $\bar{e}^2$ > OHG. *ea* > *ia* > *ie*

Goth. *hēr*	OHG. *hēr, hear, hiar, hier*
VL. *spēculum*	OHG. *spiagal, spiegel*

ia is the usual form in the ninth century though Franconian had *ie* by about 850.

(2) Gmc. $\bar{o}$ > OHG. *uo*

OE. *gōd*	OHG. *guot*
OE. *fōt*	OHG. *fuoʒ*

Alemannic usually had *ua* in the ninth century, and Bavarian still had $\bar{o}$ until the late ninth century.

(3) Gmc. *ai* before *r, w, h*, and finally > OHG. $\bar{e}$

Goth. *air* 'early'	OHG. *ēr* 'formerly'
Goth. *saiws*	OHG. *sēo*, gen. *sēwes*
Goth. *aihts*	OHG. *ēht* 'possessions'
Goth. *wai*	OHG. *wē*

ai in other positions > *ei*

Goth. *stains*	OHG. *stein*

(4) Gmc. *au* before *h* and dentals (*d, t, ʒ, s, l, n, r*) > OHG. $\bar{o}$

Goth. *hauhs*	OHG. *hōh*
Goth. *audags*	OHG. *ōtag* 'rich, happy'
Goth. *stautan*	OHG. *stōʒan*
Goth. *kaus*	OHG. *kōs* 'I chose'
L. *caulis*	OHG. *kōl* (loan-word)
Goth. *laun*	OHG. *lōn*
Goth. *auso*	OHG. *ōra*

au in other positions > *ou*

Goth. *augo*	OHG. *ouga*

(5) Gmc. *eu* before *i, j, u* in next syllable > OHG. *iu*

Gmc. **leuhtjan*   (Goth. *liuhtjan*)   OHG. *liuhten*

iu, at first a diphthong, was pronounced as a long monophthong, *ū*, by the late OHG. period (late OHG. *liute* = *lūte*). It was then available to represent the umlaut form of *ū* (see point (6) below).

Gmc. *eu* before *a, e, o* in next syllable > OHG. *eo* > *io*

Gmc. **þeuda*	OHG. *deota, diota*[1] 'people'
Gmc. **teuhan*	OHG. *zeohan, ziohan*

io is the normal form in the ninth and tenth centuries.

(6) *Umlaut*[2] or vowel modification is characteristic of all North and West Germanic languages. Phonetically it is one kind of assimilation, in which a sound influences another sound in its vicinity. Umlaut in High German consists in the fronting of back vowels and the raising of low vowels under the influence of the high front (palatal) sounds *i, j* in the following syllable (hence the more precise name *i*-umlaut). When the *i* or *j* disappeared or was weakened to *ə* (as in Middle High German) the modified vowel remained.

This process had certainly begun early, and by the beginning of the Old High German documentary period it is probable that all the low and back vowels and diphthongs (*a, ā, o, ō, u, ū, ou, uo*) had been modified, though some scholars think that umlaut was not complete until well into the Middle High German period. In Old High German texts, however, only the umlaut of *a* was regularly noted as *e* (so-called primary umlaut); the umlaut forms of other vowels (secondary umlaut) were not regularly noted[3] until the twelfth century, and even then only in the more carefully written manuscripts.

Primary umlaut: a before *i, j*, in next syllable > *e* (a close sound, sometimes written *ę* in grammars, to distinguish it from the more open Germanic *e*, which is sometimes written *ë*)

OHG. *gast*	OHG. *gesti* (plur.)
OHG. *faran*	OHG. *ferit* (3rd sing. pres. ind.)
Goth. *satjan*	OHG. *setzen*

[1] This word survives in the personal name *Dietrich*. The adjective *diutisk* (with *iu* because of *i* in the next syllable) is modern *deutsch*, meaning originally 'of the people', 'vernacular', then 'German'.

[2] The word was first used by Klopstock but it was Jakob Grimm who established it and other terms (e.g. *Ablaut, Rückumlaut, strong* and *weak* as classifications of nouns, adjectives, and verbs) in the technical vocabulary of German philology.

[3] One reason for this failure to note umlaut forms was that the Latin alphabet (cf. p. 28) had no suitable signs to note them.

Sound changes in German

This modification was prevented by certain consonantal groups, particularly in Upper German dialects: by *ht*, *hs*, consonant + *w* in all dialects; by *l* + consonant, *hh* in Upper German; by *r* + consonant, sometimes in Alemannic, always in Bavarian:

Franc.	*nahti*	*wahsit*	*garwita*	*eltiro*	*sehhit*	*wermen* (**warmjan*)
Alem.	,,	,,	,,	*altiro*	*sahhit*	*wermen, warmen*
Bav.	,,	,,	,,	,,	,,	*warmen*

Secondary umlaut: traces of this are present in Old High German; Notker (d. 1022) in particular regularly notes the umlaut of *u* as *iu*. The following survey represents the language about A.D. 1200.

a: ä (in places where primary umlaut was prevented; *ä* represents a very open sound)

> OHG. *nahti*   MHG. *nähte*
> OHG. *wahsit*   MHG. *wähset*

ā: æ (a very open sound, the long equivalent of short *ä*)

> OHG. *swāri*   MHG. *swære*
> OHG. *nāmi*   MHG. *næme* (2nd sing. past indic. of *nemen*)

Umlaut appears in the borrowed suffix *-ārius*, OHG. *-āri*, MHG. *-ære*:

> MHG. *gartenære*

o: ö   MHG. *hof*   MHG. *hövisch*
> OHG. *lohhir*   MHG. *löcher*

(IE. *o* became Gmc. *a* (Chapter 10, point (1)); further Gmc. *u* did not become *o* when followed by *i* in next syllable (Chapter 10, point (14)). Hence *ö* is comparatively rare and mostly confined to borrowings (VL. *olium*, OHG. *oli*, MHG. *öle*) and analogical forms. *Hübsch* is commoner than *hövisch* as an adjective from *hof*; the adjective from *holz* is *hülzin*.)

ō: œ   OHG. *scōni*   MHG. *schœne*
>   *hōhi*   *hœhe*
u: ü   OHG. *turi*   MHG. *türe*
>   *lugin*   *lügen* 'lie, falsehood'

Umlaut of *u* was often prevented by *lt* and *ld*:

> Gmc. **þuldjan*   MHG. *dulten*
> OHG. *sculdīg*   MHG. *schuldec*

and in Upper German often by *gg, ck, pf, tz* and, less often, by nasal + consonant:

MHG. MG. *brücke*	UG. *brugge, brucke*
drücken	*drucken*
hüpfen	*hupfen*
nützen	*nutzen*
wünne	*wunne*

ū: ǖ, written conventionally *iu* (see point (5) above):

OHG. *brūti*	late OHG. MHG. *briute*
(pl. of *brūt*)	
OHG. *krūzi*	MHG. *kriuze*
uo: üe OHG. *guotī*	MHG. *güete*
OHG. *suoʒi*	MHG. *süeʒe*
ou: öu OHG. *loubir*	MHG. *löuber*
(er) *loufit*	MHG. *löufet*

Umlaut of *ū, uo, ou* was often prevented by a labial consonant, and in other ways, especially in Upper German: UG. *rūmen, gelouben, toufen, troumen, ruochen* (NHG. *geruhen*), all originally ending in *-jan.*[1]

Apart from the more complete noting of umlaut, Middle High German vowels differ from Old High German vowels in only one important respect:

(7) Full vowels in unaccented syllables, initial, medial, and especially final, were reduced to the neutral vowel *e* (*ə*); many disappeared altogether. This process continued in Early New High German, when the dropping of final unaccented *e* became especially characteristic of Upper German:

OHG. *herza*	MHG. *herze*	NHG. *Herz*
hōhī	*hœhe*	*Höhe*
singan	*singen*	*singen*

[1] *Rückumlaut* ('reverse umlaut') is a misleading term used by Jakob Grimm. Certain weak verbs in Old and Middle High German show an infinitive with umlaut and a past tense without it: OHG. *zellen, zalta*; MHG. *hœren, hōrte*. Grimm believed that the past tense had once also had umlaut, but that this had been 'reversed' at a later stage. In fact the past tense never had umlaut: contrast infinitive **hōrjan*, MHG. *hœren* with past tense **hōrda*, MHG. *hōrte*. There were many such verbs in MHG.: e.g. *decken, dahte; grüeʒen, gruoʒte; füeren, fuorte.* Most have now been levelled out by analogy (*decken, deckte*), but a few survive: *kennen, kannte; rennen, rannte.*

108

Sound changes in German

OHG. *folgēn*	MHG. *folgen*	NHG. *folgen*
lebara	*lebere, leber*	*Leber*
framadi	*fremede, fremde*	*fremd*
lesāri	*lesære, leser*	*Leser*
zungōno (gen. pl.)	*zungen*	*Zungen*
gilouben	*gelouben*	*glauben*

A few unaccented vowels other than *e* still remain. These are usually in suffixes which once bore a secondary accent:

Königin, Freiheit, Reichtum, täglich, Sammlung.

(8) A few contractions may be noted. In particular *b, d, g* between vowels tended to disappear while the vowels coalesced:

ibi > *ī*	OHG. *gibit*	MHG. *gīt* (or *gibet*)
igi > *ī*	OHG. *ligit*	MHG. *līt* (or *ligit*)
age > *ei*	OHG. *sagēt*	MHG. *seit* (or *saget*)
ege > *ei*	MHG. *getregede, getreide*	NHG. *Getreide*

New High German accented vowels are very different both in quality and quantity from Middle High German ones. The main changes may be stated as follows (leaving aside, as usual, dialectal differences):

(9) MHG. *ei, ou, öu* > NHG. *ei (ai), au, eu (äu)*

ei > *ei (ai)*:   MHG. *stein*   NHG. *Stein*

The traditional spelling *ei* is retained to represent the more open diphthong *ai*. The spelling *ai* is only used occasionally to avoid ambiguity; contrast *Saite* (MHG. *seite* 'string of instrument') with *Seite* (MHG. *sīte*).[1]

| *ou* > *au*: | MHG. *boum* | NHG. *Baum* |
| *öu* > *eu (äu)*: | MHG. *fröude* | NHG. *Freude* |

The traditional spelling *eu* (in MHG. an alternative to *öu*) is retained to represent the new diphthong *oi* (or *oü*). The spelling *äu* is only used where a related form without umlaut exists; contrast *heute, Kreuz* with *Häute* (*Haut*), *läuft* (*laufen*). Its use is not determined by etymology; *Kreuz* and *Häute* are both umlaut forms, *heute* (OHG. *hiutu*) is not.

[1] The *ai* in *Kaiser* reflects a spelling convention of the Imperial chancery in Vienna (cf. p. 39).

109

(10) MHG. *ī, ū, iu* > NHG. *ei (ai), au, eu (äu)* (diphthongization)

ī > ei:	MHG. *mīn*	NHG. *mein*
	līp	*Leib*
ū > au:	*hūs*	*Haus*
	trūt	*traut*
iu > eu:	*niun*	*neun*
	hiute	*heute* or *Häute*
		(see above)

(11) MHG. *ie, uo, üe* > NHG. *ī, ū, ṻ* (monophthongization)

ie > ī (ie):	MHG. *tief*	NHG. *tief*
	liebe	*Liebe*

The traditional spelling *ie* is retained to represent the long monophthong *ī*.

uo > ū:	MHG. *guot*	NHG. *gut*
	ruofen	*rufen*
üe > ṻ:	*güete*	*Güte*
	füeren	*führen*

The diphthongization of *ī, ū, iu* (point (10)) began in Bavaria as early as the twelfth century, the monophthongization of *ie, uo, üe* (point (11)) began in Middle German about the same time. Both groups of new vowels were incorporated in East Middle German and hence in the standard language.

(12) Short vowels in open syllables are lengthened. (An open syllable is one not closed by a consonant: *le-* in *leben* is an open syllable, *fin-* in *finden* is a closed syllable.)

MHG. *geben*	NHG. *gēben*
bote	*Bōte*

(13) Long vowels in closed syllables are shortened.

MHG. *brāhte*	NHG. *brachte* (with short *a*)
hērlīch	*herrlich* (with short *e* and *i*)
lieht	*Licht* (with short *i*)

There are many apparent exceptions to the last two points; e.g. *Tag*, though a closed syllable, is lengthened, but by analogy with its inflected forms: *tăge > Tāge*. There are also a number of real ex-

Sound changes in German

ceptions: e.g. *got, gotes,* and *himel* retain short vowels (*Gott, Gottes; Himmel*) and the spelling is changed to indicate this.[1]

As a result of these thoroughgoing changes[2] modern German sounds very different from Middle High German. The effect of the qualitative changes is obvious. But the quantitative changes are no less important, for they have greatly changed the rhythm of the language, especially in conjunction with the reduction of unstressed vowels. OHG. *lĕsāri,* MHG. *lĕsǣre, lĕser,* NHG. *Lēser* show differences of rhythm at each stage.

A number of minor changes may be noted:

(14) *ā* after *w* or before nasals > *ō*

MHG.	*wāc*	NHG.	*Woge*
	wā		*wo*
	āne		*ohne*
	āmaht		*Ohnmacht*
	mānōt		*Monat*

(15) *e, i* before or after labials or *sch, w, l* > *ö, ü* (by lip-rounding)

MHG.	*leffel*	NHG.	*Löffel*
	schepfen		*schöpfen*
	zwelf		*zwölf*
	wirde		*Würde*
	giltig		*gültig*

But there are many exceptions: *elf* (contrast *zwölf*); *Hilfe, wirken* have outlived *Hülfe, würken.*

(16) *u, ü* before nasals > *o, ö,* especially in Middle German

MHG.	*sunne*	NHG.	*Sonne*
	sumer		*Sommer*
	münch		*Mönch*
	künnen		*können*

But there are many exceptions: *dumm, stumm, Kummer.*

Heilbronn and *Schönbrunn* show the Middle and Upper German forms respectively.

[1] Long vowels are indicated in modern German by being written double (*Saal, Waage*), by a following *h* (*sehen,* where *h* is now silent; *Jahr,* where *h* is unhistorical), by some special sign (*ie,* a traditional spelling in a new function); but many long vowels are not specially marked. Short vowels are often indicated by a following consonant group (*binden*) or double consonant (*Mitte*); but *Erde,* for example, has a long vowel despite the *rd.*

[2] The name 'New High German Vowel Shift' might be a convenient means of reference.

111

B. CONSONANT CHANGES

The Second or High German Sound-Shift[1] is the main feature differentiating the High German dialects from other Germanic languages, in particular from English, Frisian, and Low German. Indeed a High German dialect is so called because it has been affected, however little, by the Second Sound-Shift. It began in a southern dialect (Alemannic? Bavarian? Langobardic?) and spread northwards; and since it was more complete in the southern dialects than in dialects farther north, it can be used to distinguish the High German dialects from each other, both in medieval and modern times.

It probably began in the fifth century A.D. and took some three hundred years to develop, since it was still not completed when the first German documents were written (from 770 onwards). It may have some connection with the First Sound-Shift,[2] since the same kinds of consonants and shifts are involved; but its cause is just as obscure as that of the earlier shift. Its various elements are as follows:

(17) I. *p, t, k* medially or finally after vowels $>$ *ff, ʒʒ, xx* (written *ch*)

II. *p, t, k* initially, when doubled, and after consonants $>$ *pf, tz* (written *z, tz*), *kx* (written *ch, cch*)

III. *b/b, d, g/g* $>$ *p, t, k*[3]

Note: (*a*) *ff, ʒʒ, xx* are usually simplified to *f, ʒ, x* (*ch*) after a long vowel and finally.

----

[1] See p. 22 f.   [2] See p. 18 and p. 99 ff.

[3] These changes were completely realized only in Upper German, especially in Bavarian. While a full survey of dialectal differences would be out of place here, a few notes may be useful to the student of Old High German:

(*a*) *p, t, k* $>$ *ff, ʒʒ, xx* (I) and *t* $>$ *z, tz* (II) are common to all High German dialects, apart from a few common words in Middle Franconian (*that, it, hwat*).

(*b*) Upper German only: *k* $>$ *kx* (II) and *b/b, g/g* $>$ *p, k* (III). Alemannic often has *b, g* instead of *p, k* medially, especially between vowels.

(*c*) East Franconian, whose consonants are nearest to those of the MHG. literary language and modern standard German, has unshifted *k*, (II) *b, g* (III) and shifted *t* ($< d$) (III) and *pf* ($< p$) (II) in all positions in the word.

(*d*) South Rhenish Franconian has unshifted *p* and *d* initially, otherwise as East Franconian.

(*e*) Rhenish Franconian has unshifted *p* in all positions under II, except *lpf, rpf*, unshifted *d* initially, a fluctuation between *t* and *d* elsewhere under III, otherwise as East Franconian.

(*f*) Middle Franconian has unshifted *p* (under II) and usually unshifted *d* in all positions; *b, g* often appear as fricatives: *v, f; j, gh, ch*.

(*b*) *sp, st, sk, ft, ht, tr* remain unshifted: OHG. *spīwan, stēn, ist, fisk, haft, naht* (cf. Chapter 10, point (15)); OE. *getrīewe,* OHG. *gitriuwi.*

p > ff, f:	OE. *open*	OHG. *offan*	
	slǣpan	*slāfan*	
	skip	*skif*	
t > ʒʒ, ʒ	OE. *etan*	OHG. *eʒʒan*	
	lǣtan	*lāʒan*	
	hāt	*heiʒ*	
k > xx, x	OE. *macian*	OHG. *machōn*	
	sǣcan	*suochen*	
	ic	*ih*	
p > pf	OE. *pund*	OHG. *pfunt*	
	æppel	*apful*	
	helpan	*helpfan > helfan*	
	Lat. *campus*	*kampf*	
	OE. *þorp*	*dorpf > dorf*	
t > z, tz	OE. *tīen*	OHG. *zehan*	
	settan	*setzen*	
	heorte	*herza*	

k > kx:	OE. *corn*	OHG. *korn* (UG.) *chorn*	
	weccan (E.Franc.) *wecken*	*wechen, wecchen*	
	weorc	*werk*	*werch*
b/ƀ > p:	OE. *beran*	OHG. *beran* (UG.) *peran*	
	lamb (E.Franc.) *lamb*	*lamp*	
	sibb	*sibba, sippa*	*sippa*
	giefan	*geban*	*kepan*
d > t:	OE. *dōn*	OHG. *tuon*	
	biddan	*bitten*	
	hand	*hant*	
g/ǥ > k:	OE. *gōd*	OHG. *guot* (UG.) *coot, cuat*	
	hrycg (E.Franc.) *ruggi*	*rucki*	
	stīgan	*stīgan*	*stīcan*

Other consonantal changes in Old High German were:

(18) Gmc. *þ > đ > d:*	OE. *þorp*	OHG. *dorf*	
	OE. *þrie*	OHG. *drī*	
Goth. *brōþar*	OE. *brōþor*	OHG. *bruoder*	
	OE. *bæð*	OHG. *bad*	

113

This change was not complete in all High German dialects until well into the tenth century.

(19) Initial *wr-, wl-, hr-, hl-, hn-, hw-*, lost their initial *w* or *h*. The *w* had disappeared before the first documents were written, the *h* mostly before the end of the eighth century.

OE. *wrītan*, Eng. *write*	OHG. *rīȥan*	
OE. *wliti* 'face'	OHG. *(ant-)luzzi*,	NHG. *Antlitz*
Early OHG. *hrind*	OHG. (ninth	*rind*
hlūt	century)	*lūt*
hnīgan		*nīgan*
hwer		*wer*

(20) A number of assimilations: e.g. *inbiȥ* > *imbiȥ*
intfāhan > *infāhan*, *impfāhan*

We are now in a position to see the incidence of Verner's Law (Chapter 10, point (16)) or grammatical change in High German. The alternating consonants in Germanic:

$$f/b̌, b̧/d̄, x/g (\eta x/\eta g, xw/gw), s/z$$

developed in High German as follows:

$$f/b, d/t, h/g, h/ng, h/w, s/r.$$

The following pairs of Old High German words from the same root are examples: *durfan, darbēn; tōd, tōt; swehur, swigar* ('brother-in-law', 'sister-in-law'); *fāhan, fang; aha, ouwa* ('running water', 'water-meadow'); *kiosan, kuri*. But it is in the strong verbs that these alternations become clearest. There the infinitive and the singular of the past tense were originally accented on the root, while the plural of the past tense and the past participle were accented on the suffix. Hence we have in Old High German (to quote only the infinitive and past participle): *heffen (heben), gihaban; mīdan, gimitan; slahan, gislagan; fāhan, gifangan; līhan, giliwan; kiosan, gikoran*.

Most of these alternations, which were frequent in Old and Middle High German, have been levelled out in the modern language; but a few remain: *schneiden, geschnitten; ziehen, gezogen*.

No further major changes affect the High German consonants after the Old High German period. Only relatively minor changes are to be recorded from about the tenth century onwards. Some of these begin in the Old High German period but are more characteristic of Middle High German:

(21) OHG. *sk* > MHG. *sch* (probably through an intermediate stage *sx*):

OHG. *scōno*	MHG. *schōne, schōn*
OHG. *fisk*	MHG. *fisch*

(22) *b*, *d*, *g* became voiceless when final:

MHG. *sterben, starp*
vinden, vant
tage (pl.), *tac*

This distinction between voiced and voiceless plosives is retained in the modern language, but final *b*, *d*, *g* have been restored in spelling by analogy with forms which have *b*, *d*, *g* medially: *starb, fand, Tag.*

(23) *t* > *d* after *m* and *n*, less regularly after *l*, occasionally after *r*:

OHG. *rūmta*	MHG. *rūmde*
OHG. *hintar*	MHG. *hinder*
OHG. *dulten*	MHG. *dulden*
OHG. *weralti*	MHG. *werlde*

But this was not consistently carried through; and modern German has sometimes kept the *d* and sometimes restored the *t* by analogy: *räumte, Welt* (pl. *Welten*), but *dulden; hinter* but *verhindern*, where the etymological connection has been lost.

(24) A number of assimilations and dissimilations, covering the Middle and New High German periods, may be noted together here:

mb > mm:	MHG. *tump (tumber)*	NHG. *dumm*
	MHG. *zimber*	NHG. *Zimmer*
nm > mm:	MHG. *gruonmāt*	NHG. *Grummet* 'second crop for mowing'
	Lat. *cinnamum* OHG. MHG. *zinment*	NHG. *Zimmet, Zimt*
nl > ll, l:	MHG. *einlif, eilf*	NHG. *elf*
mf > nf:	OHG. *samfto*	MHG. *sanfte*
	OHG. *zumft*	MHG. *zunft*

The following changes, characteristic of New High German, had begun in the Middle High German period:

115

A short history of the German language

(25) *ʒ* and *s*: the distinction between these had disappeared by the late thirteenth century, and *s* or *ss* (and *ß*) began to replace *ʒ* and *ʒʒ* in spelling:

MHG. *haʒ, haʒʒes*	NHG. *Haß, Hasses*
MHG. *sträʒe*	NHG. *Straße*
MHG. *daʒ*	NHG. *das, daß* according to function

(26) Initial *sp-, st-, sl-, sm-, sn-, sw-* >, *schp-, scht-, schl-*, etc.

MHG. *sprechen*	NHG. *sprechen* (pron. *schprechen*)
stein	*Stein* (pron. *Schtain*)
släfen	*schlafen*
smerz	*Schmerz*
snē	*Schnee*
swach	*schwach*

The retention of the traditional spellings *sp-, st-* in a new function suggests that these groups had acquired their new value quite early, probably soon after *sk* became *sch* (point (21) above). In the Hamburg and Hanover areas of Northern Germany *sp* and *st* are still pronounced in the old way, and not as *schp, scht*.

(27) *rs, rʒ* > *rsch* medially and finally:

MHG. *hērsen, hersen*	NHG. *herrschen*
hirʒ	*Hirsch*

But exceptions are frequent:

MHG. *verse(n)*	NHG. *Ferse*

(28) A *t* or *d* was introduced into some words, especially after nasals, to facilitate pronunciation (so-called *t*-glide). In some cases the nasal disappeared by assimilation:

MHG. *nieman*	NHG. *niemand* (from inflected cases, e.g. *niemands*)
MHG. *eigenlich*	NHG. *eigentlich*
MHG. *allen halben* (dat. pl.)	NHG. *allenthalben*
MHG. *dīnen wegen* (dat. pl.)	NHG. *deinetwegen*

(29) Initial *tw-* > *zw-*:

MHG. (*ge-*)*twerc*	NHG. *Zwerg*
MHG. *twingen*	NHG. *zwingen*

Sound changes in German

(30) *w*, originally a bilabial sound like English *w* (MHG. *wīn*, compare Eng. *wine*), acquired its modern pronunciation, like English *v*.[1] The spelling was not changed.

(31) *lw, rw > lb, rb:*

MHG. *swalwe*	NHG. *Schwalbe*
MHG. *varwe*	NHG. *Farbe*

(32) *r*, originally a front trill, acquired its back uvular pronunciation in eighteenth-century cultured society in imitation of French pronunciation. From there it spread to all social classes and most dialects. Today it is heard everywhere, though the front trill is still recommended for the stage.

The use of initial capitals in German is, of course, a matter of spelling rather than of sound, but is worth noting here. Initial capitals were introduced in the sixteenth century and became widespread in the seventeenth to mark important words. In the eighteenth century the modern convention of writing all substantives (and words used as substantives) with a capital letter was established. Some nineteenth-century scholars tried to abolish this use of capitals, but met with little success, though in a few scholarly works (e.g. the *Deutsches Wörterbuch* of the Grimm brothers) their use was abandoned.

FOR FURTHER READING

Kurt Meisen, *Altdeutsche Grammatik I: Lautlehre*, 2nd edn., 1968 (Sammlung Metzler No. 2)
Blanka Horacek, *Kleine historische Lautlehre des Deutschen*, 2nd edn., 1966
Richard von Kienle, *Historische Laut- und Formenlehre des Deutschen*, 1960
Joseph Wright, *Historical German Grammar, Vol. 1: Phonology, word-formation and accidence*, 1907 (no more published)

[1] In some regions *w* is pronounced, not as a labio-dental fricative (i.e. lower lip and upper teeth, as English *v*) but as a bilabial fricative, with upper and lower lips.

117

CHAPTER 12

The forms of German

Indo-European, as we have seen,[1] had a rich variety of word-forms to express grammatical categories (number, case, tense, mood, etc.) as well as a large number of declensions for nouns and conjugations for verbs. It is by no means certain how these forms came into being, but it seems probable that at a very remote period the language consisted of full words carrying the basic sense and fixed in form, as well as a number of particles which indicated the relations between the full words. In the course of many centuries these particles coalesced with the full words to produce the richly inflected and apparently highly systematized language which comparative philologists have been able to reconstruct. This theory at any rate is consistent with the structure of nouns, adjectives, and verbs in the Indo-European languages. These can be analysed into a root which carries the basic sense (and may take on various ablaut forms; cf. Chapter 10, section B), one or more suffixes indicating the part of speech of the word and the declension or conjugation to which it belongs,[2] and an ending showing its actual function in the sentence. These elements are often far from obvious in the historical languages, as the following example shows:

IE. **dhogh-o-s*, Gmc. **dag-a-z:* Goth. *dag-s*, ON. *dag-r*, OE. *dæg*, OHG. *tag*.

The Germanic languages have tended to reverse this process. The Latin verb *amabor* expresses the basic meaning and the various grammatical categories in a single word; the word group *I shall be loved* fulfils the same function in English. Latin, we say, is a synthetic language, English an analytical one. This tendency towards analytical expression goes hand in hand with a steady reduction in the number of inflected forms; the fewer surviving forms, supported by such

---

[1] See p. 10.   [2] *Root* and *suffix* together form the stem of the word.

functional words as prepositions and auxiliary verbs, express meaning equally well. At the same time distinctions between the different declensions or conjugations have been reduced, and smaller categories, with only a few words in each, have been absorbed into the larger ones. In German, for example, the weak conjugation has absorbed a number of verbs which once were strong; and it continues to expand with the addition of new verbs.

These processes were apparently far advanced in Germanic, and by the time the first German texts were written down they had gone even further. Nor did they stop even then, for we can observe their effects with great clarity through some ten centuries. Indeed it was only by the efforts of grammarians, particularly in the sixteenth, seventeenth, and eighteenth centuries, that German acquired the fixity of form which we know today. Since the early nineteenth century only minor changes have been made in word-forms, though even today not every detail has been regulated (*dem Tag* or *dem Tage*, *gehe* or *geh*, *buk* or *backte*).

A. NOUNS

Indo-European nouns had three numbers (singular, dual, plural) and eight cases (nominative, vocative, accusative, genitive, dative, ablative, locative, instrumental). By the Germanic stage the dual had virtually disappeared; it survived only in a few pronouns. The cases were also much reduced. The vocative tended to coalesce with the nominative, and only Gothic has a few remains. The ablative had already partly coalesced with the genitive in the singular and with the dative in the plural in Indo-European; in Germanic it disappeared as a separate case. The locative, too, is unknown in the Germanic languages. The instrumental did indeed survive, but only in the West Germanic languages. Even in these it was rapidly losing its identity; in Old High German it is nearly always reinforced by the preposition *mit*. By the later ninth century it disappeared entirely, its function being taken over by the dative. A few modern forms such as *desto* and *heute* have their origin in instrumental cases.

By Old High German, then, there were two numbers and virtually four cases; and this pattern has continued to the present day. In the dialects, it is true, the genitive has largely disappeared; but it is still extensively used in the more elaborate and conservative standard language and shows little sign of disappearing.

The development of the declensions has been more complicated. Indo-European had a large number of declensions (the number differs according to how they are classified). According to the ending of the word-stem we may distinguish vocalic and consonantal declensions. Some of the latter had no formative suffix[1] but the bare root served as the stem. Such words are called root-stems. In Germanic the vocalic declensions had stems ending in *a* (= Indo-European *o*, cf. Chapter 10, point 3), *ō*, *i* and *u*; consonantal declensions were either root-stems or had stems ending in *r*, *nt*, *s*, and *n*.

In the Old High German period the *a*-stems (masculines like *tag* and neuters like *wort*), *ō*-stems (feminines like *geba*) and *i*-stems (masculines like *gast* and feminines like *kraft*) remained in full vigour. The *u*-declension, however, appears only in a few masculines such as *situ* (NHG. *Sitte*, now feminine), *fridu* (*Friede*), *sigu* (*Sieg*), and *sunu* (*Sohn*), the neuter *fihu* (*Vieh*) and the feminine *hant*; otherwise the words in this declension have been absorbed into the *a*- or the *i*-declension. The modern form *vorhanden*, containing an old dative plural (contrast dat. pl. *Händen*), is a relic of the *u*-declension.

The root-stems were also rapidly being absorbed into the *a*- or the *i*-declension, though the masculine *man* and the feminine *naht* show the declension still intact; the modern plural *Mann* ('*zwanzig Mann*') may be a relic of this. The *r*-stems are a small group of relationship names, *fater*, *bruoder*, *muoter*, *tohter*, *swester*. These, too, acquire forms from the *a*- and *ō*-declension but retain older forms throughout the period, notably – in the case of the masculines – genitive singulars without -*s*, forms still quite common in Middle High German: *des vater/vaters*, *des bruoder/bruoders* (MHG. *man* still has *des man* as well as *des mannes*). The *nt*- declension contained only two nouns, *friunt* and *fiant*, originally present participles; by late Old High German they were almost entirely assimilated to the *a*-declension. The *s*-declension contains words like *lamb*, plur. *lembir*. Here the original stem is represented by the form *lembir* (Gmc. **lambiz*), to which inflexional endings were added. Later the suffix -*ir* (-*iz*) was interpreted as a plural ending and a new shortened singular was formed (*lamb*) and declined like an *a*-stem.

The only consonantal declensions which remained in full vigour were the *n*-stems, masculines like *boto* (*Bote*), neuters like *herza* (*Herz*)

---

[1] See note 2 on p. 118 above.

and feminines like *zunga* (*Zunge*), with case-endings in *-n* in all forms except the nominative singular.[1]

The reduction of full vowels in unaccented syllables (Chapter 11, point (7)) and the consequent collapse of the system of distinctive case-endings led to much ambiguity in Middle High German. This was in practice much less disastrous than it sounds for the context usually enabled the hearer to interpret ambiguous forms correctly. Nevertheless the late Middle Ages saw many changes, some deliberately made by grammarians, others introduced less consciously by ordinary speakers, to bring out essential distinctions in the declensional systems. A few of the more important changes are described here.

The principal feminine declensions in Middle High German were:

		ō-stems	i-stems	n-stems
Sg:	N.	gebe	kraft	zunge
	A.	gebe	kraft	zungen
	G.	gebe	krefte	zungen
	D.	gebe	krefte	zungen
Pl:	N.	gebe	krefte	zungen
	A.	gebe	krefte	zungen
	G.	geben	kreften	zungen
	D.	geben	kreften	zungen

Now the essential distinction in a noun, we may suppose, is that between singular and plural. In these declensions this distinction is hardly made at all. At the same time the ō-stems and *n*-stems had common features: both had their nominative singulars in *-e* and their genitive and dative plurals in *-en*. In course of time the two declensions coalesced, the ō-stem singular and the *n*-stem plural being combined in a singular 'mixed' declension with *-e* throughout the singular and *-en* throughout the plural. In the *i*-stems the singular was levelled to a single form (*kraft*) quite early in Middle High German; and somewhat later the plural underwent some levelling (*krefte, krefte, krefte, kreften*).[2] Thus the modern situation is reached, in which feminines are uninflected in the singular and form their

[1] The vocalic declensions are sometimes called strong and the *n*-declensions weak. This distinction is useful in Old and Middle High German; but in modern German it serves only to distinguish weak masculines like *Bote* (*des Boten, die Boten*) from other masculines. No true weak neuters or feminines survive.

[2] The *-n* in the dative plural is, of course, common to all declensions and is the only feature which has remained virtually unchanged since Old High German. It is omitted only in plurals ending in *-s*: *Salons, Schupos*.

A short history of the German language

plural in a variety of ways, usually in -*en*, more rarely in -*e* with or without umlaut and – for a very few nouns – with umlaut alone (*Mütter*).

Masculine *n*-stems also failed to distinguish clearly between singular and plural. Some of these, like *Bote*, have retained their 'weak' declension and rely on the context (adjectives, articles, prepositions) to indicate the sense.[1] Under the influence of the strong declensions, others have added -*s* to the genitive singular, thus producing another type of mixed declension: *Name, des Namens, die Namen*. Some words which had adopted this change between the fifteenth and nineteenth centuries have reverted to the other pattern: *Geselle, Gatte* had genitive singulars *Gesellens, Gattens* for a time; now the normal forms are again *des Gesellen, des Gatten*. Other words conform still more closely to the *a*-stem pattern by adopting -*n* in the nominative singular as well: *Spaten, des Spatens, die Spaten* (contrast MHG. *spate, spaten, spaten*). In others there is some fluctuation between nominative singulars with or without -*n*: *Glaube* or, more rarely, *Glauben*. Finally a number of words reduce ambiguity still further by adding umlaut in the plural: *Garten, des Gartens, die Gärten* (MHG. *garte, garten, garten*).

The few neuter *n*-stems have gone different ways. *Herz* keeps the old pattern most closely (*Herz, Herz, Herzens, Herzen; Herzen* throughout plural). *Auge* and *Ohr* decline strong like *Tag* in the singular and retain the weak -*en* in the plural. *Wange* has become feminine and declines like *Zunge*.

Umlaut used alone without an inflexional ending to indicate the plural was not very characteristic of Middle High German despite the existence of *veter, brüeder, müeter, töhter*. In the modern language it is used in some words as the sole sign of the plural: *Gärten, Wässer* (but also *Wasser*). Umlaut is sometimes added even where singular and plural forms were already different: MHG. *hof*, pl. *hove*; NHG. *Hof, Höfe*. It is especially frequent along with the ending -*er*. Neuters of the type *lamp*, pl. *lember* were comparatively rare in Middle High German. Most strong neuters were of the type of *wort*, where in the nominative and accusative the singular and plural showed no distinction: *wort*, pl. *wort*, in contrast to the masculine *tac*, pl. *tage*. Such neuters have developed new plurals, many on the analogy of *Lamm* (*Schwert, Schwerter*), but some on the analogy of

[1] Some words which retain this weak declension drop the final -*e* in the nominative singular: MHG. *grave*, NHG. *Graf*.

ag (*Jahr*, *Jahre*). A small number, indeed, developed two new plurals: *Wort* still has *Worte* and *Wörter*, *Land* has *Länder* and, much more rarely, *Lande*. These alternative plurals have now developed differences of meaning.

The last examples serve to show that the developments in declensions are much more haphazard than they seem. Analogy and the desire to link ambiguous forms with established patterns are forces which do not operate systematically; and they have produced a very complicated pattern indeed. It might even be argued that there is no longer any pattern at all and that the system of German declensions is one of the least satisfactory aspects of the language.

B. PRONOUNS

Indo-European pronouns cannot be reconstructed with any confidence, since the various extant languages have such extremely varied pronominal forms. But it seems likely that there were two kinds. One group did not make distinctions of gender, but had the same forms for masculine, neuter, and feminine; these included the first and second personal pronouns (*ich*, *du*) and a pronoun which may once have been a third personal pronoun but which appears in the historical languages only as a reflexive (*sich*). The other group, which included demonstrative and interrogative pronouns, had separate forms for the three genders. The third personal pronoun (*er*, *sie*, *es*) may have been supplied by a demonstrative (i.e. 'he' was probably expressed as 'that one').

The personal pronouns, it seems, had three numbers and eight cases like nouns but differed from nouns in the fact that the eight case-forms were not inflected forms of a single root or stem. Rather several roots were represented in each pronoun. German *ich*, *mich*, *wir*, *uns*, and *du*, *ihr* seem to bear this out.

In the Germanic languages the pronouns suffered much the same reduction in the number of forms as nouns. But the dual survived longer. Old English has dual forms for all four cases in the first and second personal pronouns, and Gothic has very nearly as many. In Old High German such dual forms have virtually disappeared; the one form *unker*, which appears in Otfrid, i.e. as late as 860–70, needs the support of a numeral: *unker zweio* 'of us two'. But the modern Bavarian dialect forms *ös*, *enk* ('you', nom. acc. pl.) are relics of the dual.

A short history of the German language

The *personal pronouns* in Old High German were as follows:

	1st person	2nd person	masc.	neut.	fem.	reflexive
Sg. N.	*ih*	*dŭ*	*er*	*iʒ, eʒ*	*siu*	—
A.	*mih*	*dih*	*inan*	*iʒ, eʒ*	*sia*	*sih*
G.	*mīn*	*dīn*	—	*es*	*ira*	*sīn*
D.	*mir*	*dir*	*imu*	*imu*	*iru*	—
Pl. N.	*wir*	*ir*	*sie*	*siu*	*sio*	—
A.	*unsih*	*iuwih*	*sie*	*siu*	*sio*	*sih*
G.	*unsēr*	*iuwēr*	*iro*	*iro*	*iro*	—
D.	*uns*	*iu*	*im*	*im*	*im*	—

The missing parts of the reflexive pronoun, notably the dative, were supplied from the personal pronouns, while *sīn* was used for the genitive singular of the third personal masculine pronoun.

In the development to Middle High German and then to modern German a number of changes have occurred:

(*a*) The forms of the genitive singular *mīn*, *dīn*, *sīn* were expanded in the late Middle Ages to *mīner*, *dīner*, *sīner* (NHG. *meiner*, *deiner*, *seiner*).

(*b*) The dative plural *uns* replaces the longer accusative form *unsih*; by contrast the accusative form *euch* (*iuwih*) replaces the shorter dative form *iu*.

(*c*) The accusative reflexive *sich* (*sih*) is extended to the dative (Luther still writes: *Unser keiner lebt ihm selber*, Rom. 14, 7).

(*d*) With the loss of distinction between *ʒ* and *s* (Chapter 11 point (25)) the nominative and accusative forms *iʒ*, *eʒ* are confused with the genitive *es*; *es* becomes the nominative and accusative form.

(*e*) The distinctions between *siu* and *sia* (nom. acc. sing. fem.) and between *sie*, *siu*, *sio* (nom. acc. pl.) are lost; all are now *sie*.

(*f*) *ira*, MHG. *ir* (gen. sg. fem.) and *iro*, MHG. *ir* (gen. pl.) are replaced by *ihrer* to avoid confusion with *ihr* in the dative singular and *im*, MHG. *in* (dat. pl.) is replaced by *ihnen*, to avoid confusion with *ihn* in the accusative singular.

The possessive pronouns in Old High German were *mīn*, *dīn*, *sīn*, *unsēr*, *iuwēr*, all declined as strong adjectives.[2] Until late Middle High German there were no such pronouns for the feminine singular o

[1] See p. 139, note 3.   [2] See p. 125.

124

he plural of the third person ('her', 'their'). These were supplied by
he genitive of the appropriate personal pronoun, MHG. *ir, ir,*
iterally 'of her', 'of them'.

Of the *impersonal pronouns* the commonest in Old High German
vas the demonstrative *der*:

		M.	N.	F.			M.	N.	F.
Sg.		der	daʒ	diu	Pl.		die	diu	dio
		den	daʒ	dia			die	diu	dio
		des	des	dera			dero	dero	dero
		demu	demu	deru			dēm	dēm	dēm

his was adopted as the definite article and also as the most common
elative pronoun. Its close formal similarities to the third personal
ronouns will be clear from a comparison with the table on page 124.
To the same group belongs the interrogative pronoun *wer:*

N.	wer	waʒ
A.	wen (-an)	waʒ
G.	wes	wes
D.	wemu	wemu

Finally Old High German had a wide variety of indefinite pro-
ouns; most were compounds. Some have survived (OHG. *etteswaʒ,*
MHG. *etewaʒ,* NHG. *etwas*), some have not (OHG. *so wer so*
whoever', MHG. *swer*).

C. ADJECTIVES

n Indo-European – as, for example, in Latin – there was virtually no
difference in declension between nouns and adjectives. In Germanic
his had changed. All the Germanic languages possess two kinds of
adjective declension, called by Jakob Grimm 'strong' and 'weak'.
n Old High German the strong declension is as follows:

		M.	N.	F.
Sg.	N.	guot* / guotēr	guot* / guotaʒ	guot* / guotiu
	A.	guotan	guot* / guotaʒ	guota*
	G.	guotes*	guotes*	guotera
	D.	guotemu	guotemu	guoteru
	I.	guotu*	guotu*	—

125

Pl.		M.	N.	F.
	N.	*guote*	*guotiu*	*guoto*
	A.	*guote*	*guotiu*	*guoto*
	G.	*guotero*	*guotero*	*guotero*
	D.	*guotēm*	*guotēm*	*guotēm*
	I.	—	—	—

The endings here derive partly from *a*- or *ō*-stem nouns (these are marked with an asterisk) and partly from the impersonal pronouns. This mixture of nominal and pronominal forms was already present in Indo-European for certain adjectives (and is reflected in Latin *unus*, *solus*, *totus*, with a genitive sing. in -*ius* and a dat. sing. in -*i*). The forms without ending in the nominative singular (and neuter accusative singular) are now obsolete. They were still common in the eighteenth century, especially in the neuter, and they linger on in a few set phrases: *auf gut Glück; 'Wer da?' 'Gut Freund!'; sich lieb Kind machen.*

The strong declension of adjectives was inherited, in principle if not in all its details, from Indo-European. The weak declension is a characteristic Germanic development and is shared by all the Germanic languages. Its declension presents none of the diversity of the strong adjective, being exactly that of the weak (*n*-stem) noun, i.e. for Old High German, masculine *guoto* like *boto*, neuter *guota* like *herza*, feminine *guota* like *zunga*.[1]

The comparative of the adjective was made in Old High German by adding -*ir* or -*ōr* to the stem, the superlative by adding -*ist* or -*ōst*. -*ir* and -*ōr* are developments of two different ablaut grades of an Indo-European suffix *-ios*; -*ist* and -*ost* are further developments of the same suffix. -*ir* and -*ist* caused umlaut of the stem vowel. This explains why some adjectives have umlaut in the comparative and superlative (*lang*, *länger*, *längst*) while others do not (*froh*, *froher*, *frohst*). It should be noted, however, that the forms with or without umlaut in the modern language were not always the same ones in the older language. In Old High German comparatives and superlatives were usually declined weak.[2]

There are a few adjectives with irregular comparisons: *gut*, *besser*, *best; viel*, *mehr*, *meist.* In Old and Middle High German there were others (e.g. MHG. *übel*, *wirser*, *wirste*). In these the comparatives and superlatives are formed on different roots from the positive form; but whether these irregular comparisons simply combine the

[1] See p. 120 f.   [2] See p. 141.

relics of two adjectives of similar meaning, as has been suggested, is doubtful.

In modern German adjectives can be used in their uninflected form as adverbs. In Old and Middle High German adverbs had forms distinct from their corresponding adjectives. Most adverbs were formed by adding *-o* (MHG. *-e*) to the adjective stem: OHG. *lango* from *lang*, *scōno* from *scōni* (MHG. *lange* from *lanc*, *schōne* from *schœne*).[1] Comparatives and superlatives were in *-ōr* and *-ōst: langōr*, *langōst*. Other adverbs were formed with the suffix *-līcho:* OHG. *gernlīcho* from *gern* (though *gerno* also exists). This form still survives in *bitterlich* from adj. *bitter*. Finally the adverb corresponding to an adjective was occasionally from an entirely different root: OHG. *wola*, the adverb corresponding to *guot*.

D. NUMERALS

In Indo-European the numerals seem to have been a distinct type of word; as in later times, some were inflected and some were not. In Germanic the first four were inflected. In Old High German only the first three were normally inflected. *Ein* had the ending of a strong adjective. The forms of 'two' and 'three' have gradually been reduced in number until only the single forms *zwei* (originally neuter) and *drei* (originally masculine) are now normal in all positions, though the genitives *zweier* and *dreier* are found occasionally, as are also dative forms: *zu dreien*. The modern form *zwo* is a revival of an old feminine form. It is used when confusion of *zwei* and *drei* is possible, e.g. on the telephone, and is also heard quite often in conversation. The numerals 'four' to 'twelve' could be inflected when they were used as nouns or placed as adjectives after nouns (OHG. *mit knehton sibinin* 'with seven servants'). This practice still continues in phrases such as: *auf allen vieren*.

In OHG. *einlif* (*elf*) and *zwelif* (*zwölf*) the second element *-lif* seems to be connected with Eng. *leave*. The words would then mean 'one left over', 'two left over', i.e. after ten. 'Thirteen' to 'nineteen' were made with *-zehan* 'ten' as second element, and the tens from

[1] In modern German, the form *schon* (without umlaut) has developed the meaning 'already', while *schön* (with umlaut) now functions as both adjective and adverb 'beautiful(ly)'. *Fast* and *fest* (OHG. *fasto, festi*) show a similar development.

'twenty' to 'ninety' with -*zug: drīzehan, fiorzehan*, etc.; *zweinzug, drīẓẓug*, etc. Since *zug* was a noun meaning 'decade', the tens were for long used as nouns and followed by a genitive.

In Old High German 'hundred' was *zehanzug* 'ten tens' rather than *hunt* (< I.E. **k̑m̥tóm*), though multiples were made with *hunt: zwei hunt*, etc. This may be the result of a confusion traceable to Babylonian influence. From Babylon the Indo-European peoples learned a duodecimal system of reckoning, in which the 'hundred' seems to have meant the so-called 'great hundred' of ten twelves. By Middle High German 'hundred' was *hundert*.

Of the ordinals 'first' had two forms in Old High German, *ēristo* and *furisto* (cf. Eng. *first*), both inherited from Germanic. From Middle High German the second word has become a noun with specialized meaning: MHG. *fürste*, NHG. *Fürst*. 'Second' was represented in Germanic by 'other': OHG. *andar; zweit* does not appear until the fifteenth century.[1] The ordinals from 'third' onwards were formed from the cardinals: *dritto, fiordo*. In Old High German they were declined weak, as were *ēristo, furisto*.

E. VERBS

The Indo-European verb, like the noun, had a rich variety of forms: three persons, three numbers (like the noun), three voices (active, passive, middle), at least four moods (indicative, subjunctive, optative, imperative), and six tenses (present, imperfect, aorist, perfect, pluperfect, future), as well as a number of infinitives and participles. In the making of these forms ablaut[2] played a large part, as did a large number of suffixes and a host of inflexional endings. It is possible that the whole verbal system was rather haphazard and represented a number of overlapping patterns.

Germanic shows a drastic reduction of this system. The dual has gone in the same measure as in the noun. The middle and passive voices have also virtually disappeared, though Gothic still has a medio-passive voice in the present. The tenses have been reduced to two, a present corresponding to the Indo-European present and a past representing formally the Indo-European perfect but containing occasional aorist forms. The indicative mood remains much as before, but the optative has taken over the functions of the sub-

[1] See pp. 41–2 and 89.　　　　[2] See p. 98 f.

junctive and is itself usually called the subjunctive (or conjunctive) in grammars of the Germanic languages. The imperative survives in a greatly reduced form. In the formation of verbal stems ablaut has come to play a dominant role.

The new feature in the Germanic verbal system, however, is the emergence of weak verbs – the term is again Jakob Grimm's – organized in an entirely different way from the so-called strong verbs inherited from Indo-European. Whereas in the strong verb the present and past tenses and the past participle are distinguished from each other by ablaut variants of the stem vowel, the weak verb forms its past tense and past participle by means of dental suffixes (i.e. suffixes containing *t* or *d*): contrast Eng. *sing, sang, sung* with *love, loved, loved* or Ger. *binden, band, gebunden* with *sagen, sagte, gesagt*. The dental suffix is probably connected with the verb 'to do' (Eng. *do*, Ger. *tun*) and this weak conjugation may have been present in embryo in Indo-European (cf. the Latin participle *ama-t-us*); but nowhere else has it developed so elaborately as in Germanic. The strong conjugation acquires no new verbs except by analogy (e.g. *schreiben*, from Lat. *scribere*, became strong by analogy with *reißen*, which it replaced in the sense of 'write'); in principle all new verbs are weak.

In Gothic (as in Germanic) some verbs formed their past tenses with the help of reduplication, i.e. by repeating the initial consonant of the stem: Goth. *haitan* 'to be called', past *haíhait* (pron. *hehait*). These reduplicated forms do not survive in North or West Germanic languages. The West Germanic languages, again, have one small but important feature which distinguishes them from both North Germanic and Gothic. The second person singular of the past indicative of strong verbs does not have the same stem as the first and third persons but rather the stem of the plural and an ending which goes back to the Indo-European aorist (not the perfect): contrast OE. *gēafe* 'thou gavest' with first and third persons *geaf*, or OHG. *gābi* with *gab*. Gothic and Old Icelandic have *gaft*, with stem of singular and old perfect ending. This mysterious anomalous form is not replaced by a form with the usual -*st* ending of the second person singular until late in the Middle High German period: MHG. *gæbe* 'thou gavest', later *gæbst, gabst*.

The Old High German verb had only a present and a past indicative and subjunctive in the active voice, a minimal imperative, an infinitive (present) and two participles (present and past) – in short, a much reduced system, though no doubt one capable of further reduction still.[1]

The *strong verbs* fall into seven main classes as follows (Old High German forms):

		Pres. infin.	1 sg. past	1 pl. past	past part.
I	a	*strītan*	*streit*	*stritum*	*gistritan*
	b	*līhan*	*lēh*	*liwum*[2]	*giliwan*[2]
II	a	*biogan*	*boug*	*bugum*	*gibogan*
	b	*ziohan*	*zōh*	*zugum*[2]	*gizogan*[2]
III	a	*bintan*	*bant*	*buntum*	*gibuntan*
	b	*helfan*	*half*	*hulfum*	*giholfan*
IV		*neman*	*nam*	*nāmum*	*ginoman*
V		*geban*	*gab*	*gābum*	*gigeban*
VI		*graban*	*gruob*	*gruobum*	*gigraban*
VII	a	*heizan*	*hiaz*	*hiazum*	*giheizan*
	b	*loufan*	*liof*	*liofum*	*giloufan*

When the stem vowels in these classes are traced back to Indo-European it will be found that Classes I to V are based on the same ablaut series *e: o: ē: –*. The differences are due to the different vowels and consonants which follow the main vowel (n = nasal, l = liquid, k = consonant of another kind):

I	*ei*	*oi*	?	*i*
II	*eu*	*ou*	?	*u*
III	*enk/elk*	*onk/olk*	??	*ṇk/ḷk*
IV	*en/el*	*on/ol*	*ēn/ēl*	*ṇ/ḷ*
V	*ek*	*ok*	*ēk*	*(ek)*

The forms represented by question marks may well have been *ēi, ēu* and *ēnk/ēlk*, which would have conformed to the general pattern; but by Germanic times analogical forms from the past participle seem to have been substituted. The form *(ek)* in Class V has not been fully explained; it may have been some sort of neutral vowel *ə*.

Class VI is based on a number of ablaut series which have coalesced in Germanic into *a: ō: ō: a*. Class VII, sometimes called the 'reduplicating' class, is not Indo-European in origin, but contains verbs which once showed reduplication in their past tense.[3]

[1] Modern English has reduced further still. An English verb has normally only five forms in all: *give, gives, gave, giving, given.*
[2] For the consonants in these forms see p. 102 and p. 114 (grammatical change).
[3] Examples of the development of strong verbs are given in more detail in Appendix I, p. 147.

The forms of German

These classes of strong verbs are still recognizable in Middle High German. In modern German analogical formations have made them much less recognizable. The most far-reaching change has been the removal of the difference between singular and plural stems in the past indicative. This was usually complete by the middle of the seventeenth century. In Class I levelling went in favour of the plural vowel, either lengthened or unlengthened (*stritt, stritten; lieh, liehen*); otherwise confusion would have arisen – and in some cases did arise – with the new diphthong in the present (*streiten; leihen*).[1] In Class II ō became normal in both types (*bog, bogen; zog, zogen*); but certain verbs shortened the vowel by analogy with the past participle (MHG. *gōȝ, guȝȝen, gegoȝȝen*, NHG. *goß, gossen, gegossen*). In Class III, *a* became normal (*band, banden; half, halfen*). In Classes IV and V the lengthening of short vowels in open syllables obliterated the differences. In Classes VI and VII such differences had never existed.

The *weak verbs* show a much simpler pattern. In Old High German there were three classes, whose infinitives ended in *-en* (reduced from *-jan*, which had caused the doubling of the preceding consonant and umlaut[2]), *-ōn, -ēn*:

I	*zellen*	*zalta/zelita*	*gizalt/gizelit*
	hōren	*hōrta*	*gihōrt*
II	*salbōn*	*salbōta*	*gisalbōt*
III	*habēn*	*habēta*	*gihabēt*

By the familiar processes of reduction and elimination of unaccented vowels these classes had been reduced by Middle High German to a single class. Throughout the history of German this class has continued to grow by the incorporation of all new verbs. Indeed some verbs which were once strong have become weak: *hinken, bellen, salzen*.

As regards verb endings, apart from the replacement of the anomalous form in the second person singular of the strong past indicative,[3] only comparatively minor changes have taken place since Old High German. The long forms of the first person plural of the present indicative (*wir nemamēs, zellemēs*) were replaced in the ninth century by shorter forms taken from the subjunctive

[1] A distinction between present and past is important in the verb just as one between singular and plural is important in the noun; see section A, p. 121 above.
[2] See p. 103, point (20) and p. 106, point (6); cf. also note on *Rückumlaut*, p. 108.
[3] See p. 129.

131

(*nemēm, zellēm*, NHG. *nehmen, zählen*). The historical forms in -*s* in the second person singular (*nimis, zelis*) were replaced by forms in -*st* (*nimist, zelist*, NHG. *nimmst, zählst*), at first probably in the inverted form (*nimis du*?). The useful distinction between indicative and subjunctive in the third person plural of the present (OHG. indic. *nemant*, subj. *nemēn*; MHG. *nement, nemen*) has been lost (NHG. both *nehmen*). In Old High German the infinitive, being functionally a noun, had inflected genitive and dative forms: *neman, nemannes, nemanne*. The genitive form remains in modern German, where in principle every infinitive may be used as a noun: *das Singen, des Singens*. The dative form was chiefly used after the preposition *zu*: *zi nemanne*. By the late fourteenth century this form had been shortened to one indistinguishable from the basic form of the infinitive, and the awareness of its nominal function was thus lost: *zu nehmen*.

A small but important group of verbs are the *preterito-present* verbs, so called because their present tense, though present in meaning, has the form of a strong past tense: OHG. *darf, darft, darf; durfum, durfut, durfun* (compare *half, hulfi, half; hulfum, hulfut, hulfun*; but note the -*t* of the original perfect in *darft*, in contrast to the anomalous 'aorist' form *hulfi*). The weak past tenses are new Germanic formations. An explanation of these verbs is that their present tenses were once past tenses of a kind which could readily develop a present meaning. In *ih weiz*, connected with Latin *vidi* 'I have seen' the transition is plausible enough: 'I have seen', therefore 'I know'. But the explanation is somewhat less obvious for other members of the group: *ih darf, mag, muoʒ, kan, scal*, also *ih an, gi-an* (NHG. *gönne*, now weak) *gitar* 'dare' (now extinct), *iʒ toug* 'it is worth, useful' (*taugen*, now weak) and the defective verb *wir eigun* 'we have'. Another explanation is that the Indo-European perfect expressed not only an action in the past but the present state to which the action has led.

The verb *wollen* tends to be associated with this group; but its OHG. infinitive *wellen* and the present tense *willu, wili, wili, wellemēs, wellet, wellent* indicate a quite different and probably a mixed origin. The forms of the singular suggest old optative forms; the plural is that of a simple weak verb. The later development has been influenced by *sollen*.

Finally we may mention the so-called *mi*-verbs. This group, which was of considerable size in Indo-European, is represented in Old

High German by *ih bim* 'I am', *tuon* 'to do', the short forms *gān/gēn* and *stān/stēn* (corresponding to the strong *gangan* 'go' and *stantan* 'stand'). These verbs, despite wide differences, are similar in that the first person singular of the present indicative ends in a nasal: *bim/bin, tuom/tuon, gān, stān*. The nasal is the remains of the Indo-European ending *-mi*. In contrast verbs not in this group ended in *-ō* at this point (cf. Gk. *luō* 'I loose', *eimi* 'I am'). This *-ō* became *-u* in Old High German (*hilfu*) and has been *-e* since Middle High German. The nasal ending was adopted by weak verbs in Classes II and III: *ih salbōm, habēm*. Today only *ich bin* still has the old nasal ending.

The great weakness of the much reduced Old High German verbal system was its lack of variety and subtlety in expression. While a simple present (also used to express the future) and a simple past (also used for perfect and pluperfect) in the active voice only will go a long way in ordinary colloquial speech, a time comes when one needs to express the future, the perfect, the pluperfect, and the passive more precisely. For scholars nourished on the elaborate verbal system of Latin, as the earliest writers of German were, this time must have come quite early. Much of the impulse to invent compound forms in German (i.e. forms made by combining participles or infinitives with auxiliary verbs) probably came from Latin, or from the *lingua romana*, the forerunner of French, which was itself beginning to develop compound tenses.

For the perfect, the present of *habēn* and *sīn* combined with the past participle goes back to Old High German. *Eigun* was also used, as were also forms of *wesan* (a verb meaning 'to be' which is still represented by *war, gewesen*). The pluperfect was expressed in the same way by using the past tense of the auxiliary. Another way of expressing the pluperfect was by combining the prefix *ge-* with the past tense of the verb: MHG. *ich gesach* can mean 'I had seen', though indeed it has other meanings as well, since *ge-* has various functions.

The new future tense evolved slowly. To render the Latin future, Old High German translators sometimes used the present tense of *wollen* and *sollen* (compare the use of *will* and *shall* in English) and even *müssen* with the present infinitive; these are basically verbs expressing volition and obligation. In Middle High German a combination of the present tense with *ge-* is frequent: *ich gesihe* 'I begin to see' leads to the meaning 'I shall see'. All of these, however, were displaced by *werden*. The future meaning probably arose first in

A short history of the German language

phrases such as *ich wirde sehende*, constructed on the model of *ich wirde alt*. The present participle is then shortened to a form identical with the infinitive;[1] hence the modern standard form *ich werde sehen*, which was established only in the sixteenth century.

To express the passive Old High German writers used the present of both *werdan* and *wesan* with the past participle; the former was fairly widespread by the end of the period. In Middle High German the normal distinction is: *wirde* and *wart* express present and past, *bin* and *was* express perfect and pluperfect; and this usage is still found in some regions. But perfect and pluperfect passives of the type *ich bin geliebt worden, ich war geliebt worden* were also possible, and these have become normal in the standard language.

But this discussion of compound tenses has already led away from the forms of words and into the field of syntax, of the relationship of words to each other. This will be the topic in the final chapter.

FOR FURTHER READING

Kurt Meisen, *Altdeutsche Grammatik II: Formenlehre*, 2nd edn., 1968 (Sammlung Metzler No. 3)
See also books by von Kienle and Wright on p. 117

[1] Compare the reduction of *zi nemanne* to *zu nehmen* above, p. 132.

CHAPTER 13
Syntax

Syntax deals, not with the forms of individual words, but with their function in connected speech and their relationships in the sentence. Form and function are closely connected and often influence each other, as the last paragraphs of Chapter 12 have shown. Having lost all but a few inflected verbal forms, German has replaced the lost forms with syntactical devices, by combining words (auxiliary verbs, infinitives, participles) to function in groups. This tendency to make up for deficiencies by inventing new syntactical devices is one which can be seen at all stages in German.

The study of Indo-European syntax has yielded comparatively few agreed results. The language seems to have had all the parts of speech we know from the historical languages, with the exception of the article. It had sentences expressing statements, questions, and commands; and it seems to have had complex sentences with subordinate clauses, though no subordinating conjunctions have been reconstructed. As a highly inflected language it probably had great freedom in its word-order, as was still the case, for example, in Latin; but the use to which the freedom was put, being a matter of style rather than of grammar, is unknown to us.

By Germanic times sentence structure had become more complex. Indirect speech was possible, with a so-called sequence of tenses. Germanic may also have developed a dative absolute construction corresponding to the ablative absolute in Latin and the genitive absolute in Greek; but whether this was a spontaneous development or an imitation of the classical languages is not clear.

Even in the historically attested languages the ambiguities remain. Ulfilas's Gothic,[1] which is virtually the only Gothic we know, was much influenced by Greek, and it is often doubtful whether some feature of Gothic syntax is a native growth or Greek syntax in

[1] See pp. 21 and 27.

disguise. Similarly the earliest written German, especially the prose, consisted mainly of translations or adaptations of Latin texts and was much influenced by the Latin in whose study the writers and scribes had learnt their skills. The appearance, for example, of a dative absolute or of an accusative and infinitive construction and the tendency to construct more complex sentences are either due to a direct imitation of Latin or are greatly encouraged by Latin models. Much later, in the fifteenth and sixteenth centuries, Latin influence again became dominant. The categories and technical terms normally used in German grammar are still largely Latin. The tendency to place the verb at the end of the sentence or clause – a practice which has become a fixed rule for subordinate clauses in modern German – was probably Germanic or even Indo-European in origin; but it was greatly strengthened by Latin usage and by the precepts of grammarians trained in Latin. To Latin we owe a variety of un-German participial constructions (*Nach genommenem Abschied von seinem Freund*, Schiller). And we must lay at least some of the blame on Latin for the practice of incapsulation (*ein mit Moos bedeckter Stein*), a construction whose admirable economy of words can lead to obscurity when used to excess.[1]

A. SENTENCE STRUCTURE

The shape of the simple sentence or main clause is chiefly determined by the position of the verb. In Germanic, as in Indo-European, there seems to have been much freedom. The verb could be either the first or the second or the last element[2] in the sentence, the beginning and (possibly to a lesser degree) the end of the sentence being the emphatic positions. Both the initial and the final positions were quite common in simple statements in Old High German; but by Middle High German the modern usage, in which the verb is second element, was becoming firmly established. With the increased use of pronoun subjects the initial use became less common: where it might have remained, a false subject *eʒ* (cf. NHG. *Es kam der Tag, wo . . .*) or the adverb *dō* (NHG. *da*) preceded the verb. The old usage survives

[1] The influence of Vulgar Latin or the early Romance languages may have been at work in the development of compound verbal forms (see p. 133), and of pronoun subjects (p. 142).
[2] *Element* is not, of course, the same as *word*. The verb may still, for example, be second element even when it is preceded by a phrase or a subordinate clause: *erst nach drei Stunden kam der Arzt*.

in phrases like *Weiß Gott* or, for example, in *Sah ein Knab ein Röslein stehn*, where Goethe deliberately intends an archaic, folk-song effect. The final position was also abandoned by the mid-eleventh century except in imitation of Latin style or for archaic effects. The modern rule that infinitives and participles used as components of compound tenses stand at the end of the sentence is probably a relic of this usage.

In subordinate clauses, on the other hand, the final position of the verb is retained and has become normal. By the mid-eleventh century it was becoming normal for the finite part of compound tenses to occupy the absolute final position and to be preceded by the infinitive or participle, as is the rule today. There is one common but comparatively modern relaxation of this rule. When the finite part accompanies two infinitives, it may – but need not – stand before both infinitives: *weil er ihn wird einladen wollen*. This is also allowed when one 'infinitive' is really a past participle in the form of an infinitive: . . . *weil er ihn hat einladen wollen*, . . . *weil ich ihn habe kommen sehen*.

As regards subordinating conjunctions and similar words, many changes in usage have taken place since the Middle Ages. One example must stand for many. MHG. *ob* is generally used for 'if' in conditional clauses: *waʒ vrumt ob ich dir mēre sage* 'what good will it do if I tell you more'. Today it is replaced by *wenn*; but it is still used, as it was in Middle High German, to introduce indirect questions: *Ich weiß nicht, ob du das schon weißt.*

B. ARTICLES

How far the articles had developed in Germanic we cannot say. By Old High German they were widely used, but there is considerable variation in their usage. The definite article *der* developed from a demonstrative, and in Old High German – and even in modern German – it retains something of its demonstrative function. It refers to a specific person or thing, either one already mentioned or about to be mentioned or one well known to the hearer. But this usage did not become normal until Middle High German; Latin models, which had no article, may have retarded the development. In particular, words for unique individuals, e.g. OHG. *erda* 'the earth', *truhtin* 'the Lord' (in the religious sense), were often used without articles until quite late.

The indefinite article, which appears much less frequently in Old High German than the definite article, developed from the cardinal number 'one'. It was used to refer to an individual member of a group. Until late Middle High German it could also be used in the plural to mean 'some': OHG. *in einēn buochon* 'in some books'. Used with weak endings it meant 'only, alone': contrast OHG. *ein got* 'one God' and *eino got* or *got eino* 'the one God', 'God alone'. The modern *allein*, i.e. *ein* strengthened by the prefix *all-*, represents this stage.

In course of time the articles have acquired many other functions. The definite article, for instance, is introduced when the name of an individual is used to indicate the class to which the individual belongs (*der Mensch* 'Man') and frequently also with abstract nouns (*die Tugend* 'virtue'). But the modern rules for the use and omission of articles are very complicated – and different in many respects from English – and can hardly be reduced to a simple formula.

C. NOUNS

As we have seen, the Old High German noun had already lost the vocative, ablative, and locative cases and was rapidly losing the instrumental. The functions of these cases were taken over by surviving cases, the vocative by the nominative and the others chiefly by the dative. An ever increasing range of meaning came to be expressed by a wide variety of prepositions, which normally governed either the dative or the accusative case. The use of the prepositions has not changed very greatly since Middle High German, though some prepositions have virtually disappeared, at least from the literary language (*sonder, ab*), others now govern a different case (*gegen*, which usually took the dative in Middle High German, now takes the accusative) and still others have developed since the sixteenth century from nouns (*trotz, wegen, statt, mittels, kraft*) and other parts of speech (*während* arose from participial phrases such as *währendes krieges* 'while the war continues').

Perhaps the most interesting change in the use of cases since Middle High German is the rapid disappearance of the genitive, not indeed in the literary language (though even here its use is more restricted), but in most dialects. It is replaced by *von* with the dative or by some other syntactical device; *das Haus des Vaters*, for example, is replaced in some dialects by *dem Vater sein Haus*. This decay of the genitive is surprising in view of its widespread use in Middle High German. In addition to its possessive and partitive[1] uses, which we still know (*das Haus meines Vaters; ein Teil seines Landes*[2]) it was used to denote the material from which an object was made (*ein brünne rōtes goldes* 'a breast-plate of red gold', now normally . . . *aus rotem Golde*), and with words denoting measures (*ein trunc waʒʒers*), where apposition is now normal except where an adjective is present (*eine Flasche Wein, eine Flasche guten Weins*). With interrogative and indefinite pronouns the genitive was widespread: *iemen armer liute, waʒ mannes, vil süeʒer fröuden, genuoc der ēren, niht schœnes* (contrast the modern equivalents *irgendwelche arme Leute, was für ein Mann, viele süße Freuden, Ehre genug, nichts Schönes*). The development of the last phrase shows clearly the interrelation between form and function. In MHG. *niht schœnes* the adjective in the genitive is dependent on the pronoun *niht*; hence, for example, *mit niht schœnes*. When *s* and *ʒ* ceased to be distinguished (Chapter 11, point (25)) the strong nominative (and accusative) neuter form *schœneʒ* and the genitive *schœnes* were indistinguishable. *Niht schœnes* was now interpreted as a pronoun with a strong adjective in apposition; hence the modern forms *nichts Schönes* and *mit nichts Schönem*.[3]

The genitive was also widespread in an adverbial function: MHG. *maneger hande* 'in many ways'. This use survives in a number of adverbs ending in -*s: morgens*,[4] *rechts, vergebens, keineswegs*, and in a few set phrases: *guten Mutes, guter Dinge*. It was probably this adverbial use ('in respect of', 'as regards') which lay behind the use of the genitive after comparatives (*dicker eines dūmen* 'thicker by a thumb's breadth') and interjections (*wol mir mīner vrouwen* 'how happy I am because of my lady').

Finally it seems to have been either the adverbial or the partitive function which lay behind the use of the genitive after verbs. Such verbs were very numerous and included common words like *beginnen, bitten, empfinden, genießen, mangeln, pflegen, schonen, sterben,*

---

[1] i.e. denoting a whole of which a part is expressed in the governing word.

[2] For constructions with the genitive when it was placed before the governing noun see p. 60 f.

[3] A similar development is seen in *ich bin es satt*. In MHG. *ich bin es sat*, the *es* is genitive dependent on the adjective *sat*. When genitive *es* and nominative/accusative *eʒ* ceased to be distinguished, *es* was interpreted as accusative. Hence it is now possible to say *ich bin die Sache satt* (though the genitive *der Sache* is also possible).

[4] *Nachts* is formed by analogy; *Nacht* never had a genitive in -*s*.

vermissen, wünschen. In some cases the genitive was still found in the early nineteenth century, but it has now been replaced by a direct object in the accusative or by a prepositional phrase (*bitten um, mangeln an, sterben an*). Some adjectives were also followed by the genitive: *arm* (now *arm an*), *frei* (now *frei von*), *froh* (now *froh über*), to name but a few examples.

D. ADJECTIVES

In modern German only attributive adjectives are inflected, while predicative adjectives have no inflexion: *ein guter Mann* but *der Mann ist gut*. In Germanic, as in Latin, predicative adjectives, including participles, were inflected, but by Old High German there was considerable confusion between inflected and uninflected forms, participles being the first to reject inflexion. By Middle High German only a few instances remained (*sīn jāmer wart so vester* 'his grief became so great'). Today the rule that predicative adjectives are uninflected is invariable.

The attributive adjective in Old High German could be placed either before or after its noun, apparently with no difference in meaning. By Middle High German this freedom had been restricted and apart from a few cases which survived apparently for special reasons (e.g. *der künec guot* to give a rhyme) the present rule that attributive adjectives precede their noun had been established. The older usage survives in the set phrase *mein Vater selig* 'my late father'.

We have seen[1] that one of the important innovations in Germanic was the development of a weak declension of adjectives alongside the strong one. The weak adjective was used to indicate a definite person or thing, one that has been or is about to be mentioned or one that is familiar; the strong adjective indicated less definite or familiar persons or things. In a period before the development of definite and indefinite articles (which later acquired very similar functions) this was a useful distinction and it is still found to some extent in Old High German: the strong form *guot man* or *guotēr man* 'a good man' is opposed to the weak form *guoto man* 'the good man'. Otfrid has *fon himilisgen liohte* 'from the heavenly light' (with a weak adjective).

This function of the weak adjective to express definiteness is seen

[1] On pp.18 and 126.

140

Syntax

in its use with the vocative, by which a definite individual is addressed. This use is still found in Middle High German, occasionally in the singular (*liebe vater*), more frequently in the plural (*lieben brüeder*); indeed such weak adjectives with vocative plurals are still found in the nineteenth century. The comparative and superlative grades, which also imply definite individuals, were also normally declined weak in Old High German; but by Middle High German they were declined both strong and weak like other adjectives.

In modern German strong and weak adjectives are used according to mechanical rules of grammar, the weak form being used after (strong) inflected forms of the articles or of similar words such as *dieser, jener, jeder, kein,* the strong form in other circumstances: *der gute Mann, ein guter Mann, gute Leute.* The transition from the old functional usage to the modern mechanical one has been accompanied by much inconsistency and uncertainty from Old High German onwards. Even today some fluctuation exists; for example, after indefinite adjectives like *viele* or *einige* either strong or weak adjectives may be used.

In the genitive singular of masculine and neuter nouns the strong adjective in *-es* is replaced by a form in *-en* (identical with the weak form): *guten Mutes, reinen Herzens.* This was probably done for euphony, to avoid the two hissing *s*-endings. This practice began in the seventeenth century and has now become normal, though not yet entirely invariable: *reines Herzens,* for example, is also permissible.

E. VERBS

Continuous verbal forms of the type *am going, was going* are found in all the older Germanic languages; but it is only in English that they have survived as normal forms. In Old High German they are found frequently, probably under the influence of Latin, there are examples in Middle High German (*mit klage ir helfende manec vrouwe was* 'many ladies were helping her to lament') and even a few as late as the nineteenth century: *du bist nachdenkend; etwas, dessen er sich durchaus nicht vermutend war* (Raabe). Today this construction has entirely disappeared. Phrases such as *es ist auffallend, sie ist anziehend* are quite different; in these the participle is used simply as an adjective without verbal force.

Sentences of the type *ich habe es tun können, er hat mich kommen*

141

A short history of the German language

sehen, wir haben ihn gehen lassen, in which the past participle of the modal auxiliary or of *sehen, lassen* and other verbs is replaced by a form identical with the infinitive when another infinitive is dependent on them are not found before the thirteenth century. They probably arose first in the case of *lassen,* whose past participle in Middle High German had a form *lāʒen* (without the prefix *ge-*) which was misinterpreted as an infinitive. Other verbs then substituted infinitives for past participles by analogy. Once established, the usage spread rapidly. Today it is normal for *dürfen, können, mögen, müssen, sollen, wollen,* usual but not compulsory for *lassen,* common for *sehen, hören, helfen, heißen,* and rather less common for *lehren, lernen.*

In Indo-European (as, for example, in Latin and Germanic) the person and number of the verb as well as its tense and mood were expressed by the inflected form of the verb itself. There was therefore no need to use personal pronouns as subjects of verbs when there was no noun as subject. Pronoun subjects may first have been used for emphasis, as was the case in Latin. But as inflexional endings were reduced ambiguity arose and pronoun subjects became more necessary. In Old High German they were still frequently omitted. But Middle High German was already very close to the modern language, in which pronoun subjects are normal.

Negation is expressed in Old High German by *ni* and in Middle High German by *ne* (often reduced to *en, n*): OHG. *ih ni weiʒ,* MHG. *ich enweiʒ, ichn weiʒ.* To give emphasis to the negative sense OHG. *niwiht,* MHG. *niht* was often added: MHG. *ichn weiʒ niht.* In Middle High German, as in the colloquial language and the dialects today, it was common to have two or even three negatives in a sentence or clause; these negatives did not cancel each other out but supported each other. Since the seventeenth century the literary language, chiefly under the influence of Latin, has avoided this double or triple negation, and *nicht,* originally only a supplementary negative particle, has become the normal form of negation.

Perhaps the most far-reaching changes in the syntax of verbs since Old High German have occurred in the use of the subjunctive mood. The Germanic subjunctive represents both the Indo-European optative, expressing wishes (cf. *Es lebe der König!*), and the Indo-European subjunctive proper, expressing doubt, unreality, opinion as opposed to fact, and the like. Many uses of the German subjunctive have remained constant throughout its history (e.g. in con-

142

ditional clauses: *wenn ich ihn gesehen hätte* . . . etc.). But there are a
number of differences between older usage (Middle High German)
and modern usage. For example, in a clause after an imperative or
after a comparative the subjunctive was obligatory: *seht waʒ man
mir ēren biete* 'see what respect they show me'; *diu krōne ist elter
danne der künec Philippes sī* 'the crown is older than King Philip is'.
In these cases the indicative is sufficient in modern German.

In indirect or reported speech the old sequence of tenses (present
subjunctive after a present tense in the main clause, past subjunctive
after a past tense), which is characteristic of the older language and
remained normal until late in the Middle Ages, has been replaced in
the modern literary language by a different principle. After a present
tense in the main clause the subjunctive is often replaced by the
indicative: *er glaubt, daß es Zeit ist* (or *sei*). After a past tense in a
main clause there is a tendency for the tense of the subordinate subjunctive to represent the tense of the indicative in the original statement: *er glaubte, daß es Zeit sei*, or even (though less commonly) for
the indicative to be substituted: *er glaubte, daß es Zeit war*. When
the subjunctive is used there is much freedom to choose tenses which
give forms that are distinct from the indicative. In short there is in
German – as there has been for much longer in English – a tendency
to avoid the subjunctive, either by substituting periphrastic forms
with *sollen, wollen*, and other auxiliary verbs or by simply using the
indicative. To foreign students who have learned elaborate rules for
the German subjunctive some examples of this trend are quite
startling. *Als er erkannte, sie ist tot* . . . 'when he realized she was
dead' is not the work of an illiterate but of a well-known professor
(speaking in an interview). It remains to be seen how far this flight
from the subjunctive will go and what effect it will have on the
literary language.

A short chapter such as this on German syntax cannot be ex-
haustive. We have excluded all matters of style, which is a subject
for a separate study. And within the field of grammar we have
chosen only a few topics from the many possible ones – and these
have been treated with the utmost brevity. The chapter must be
regarded as no more than an appetizer. Indeed, it has been one of
our chief aims throughout the book to awaken the reader's interest,
in the hope that he may wish to go further and deeper into the
subject. For that he must now turn to the larger handbooks and
studies which we have listed in the bibliography. There he will find

abundant material for a more elaborate study of the long, complex, and fascinating history of the German language.

FOR FURTHER READING

Hermann Paul, *Mittelhochdeutsche Grammatik*. 20th edn. by Hugo Moser and Ingeborg Schröbler, 1969
Ingerid Dal, *Kurze deutsche Syntax*, 1952
William B. Lockwood, *Historical German syntax*, 1968

Appendices

Development of strong verb classes

This table illustrates the development of strong verbs (cf. Chapter 12, p. 130). The reader may also find it useful as a résumé of the main sound changes which occurred in the development from Indo-European to modern German (cf. Chapters 10 and 11). The Indo-European and Germanic forms are, of course, hypothetical; it is doubtful if all of them actually existed in the form given here, i.e. as complete words with stem and ending. Most Indo-European perfect tenses (from which the Germanic past tenses developed) had reduplicated forms, e.g. *stestroidha, *dedouka, *bhebhondha. In most cases these forms were lost at an early stage in Germanic, but a few survived in Gothic (cf. Class VII below).

Class VII is given in a different pattern from the others. Only in Gothic do the verbs in this class represent a direct development from Indo-European; in the West (and North) Germanic languages they are assimilated to the pattern of other strong verbs and form their past tense by means of a change in the stem vowel.

	Infinitive	Preterite Singular	Preterite Plural	Past Participle
CLASS I				
IE.	*streidhonom	*stroidha	*stridhme	*stridhonos
Gmc.	*striđanam	*straiđa	*striđum	*striđanaz
OHG.	strītan	streit[1]	stritum	gistritan
MHG.	strīten	streit	striten	gestriten
NHG.	streiten	stritt	stritten	gestritten
CLASS II				
IE.	*deukonom	*douka	*dukme	*dukonos
Gmc.	*teuhanam	*tauha	*tuhum	*tuhanaz
OHG.	ziohan[2]	zōh[1]	zugum	gizogan
MHG.	ziehen	zōch	zugen	gezogen
NHG.	ziehen	zog	zogen	gezogen

147

CLASS III(a)

IE.	*bhendhonom	*bhondha	*bhn̥dhme	*bhn̥dhonos
Gmc.	*bendanam	*banda	*bundum	*bundanaz
OHG.	bintan	bant	buntum	gibuntan
MHG.	binden	bant	bunden	gebunden
NHG.	binden	band	banden	gebunden

CLASS III(b)

IE.	*kelbonom	*kolba	*kl̥bme	*kl̥bonos
Gmc.	*helpanam	*halpa	*hulpum	*hulpanaz
OHG.	helfan²	half	hulfum	giholfan
MHG.	helfen	half	hulfen	geholfen
NHG.	helfen	half	halfen	geholfen

CLASS IV

IE.	*nemonom	*noma	*nēmme	*nm̥onos
Gmc.	*nemanam	*nama	*nǣmum	*numanaz
OHG.	neman²	nam	nāmum	ginoman
MHG.	nemen	nam	nāmen	genomen
NHG.	nehmen³	nahm	nahmen	genommen

CLASS V

IE.	*ghebhonom	*ghobha	*ghēbhme	*ghebhonos
Gmc.	*gebanam	*gaba	*gǣbum	*gebanaz
OHG.	geban²	gab	gābum	gigeban
MHG.	geben	gap	gāben	gegeben
NHG.	geben³	gab	gaben	gegeben

CLASS VI

IE.	*ghrobhonom	*ghrōbha	ghrōbhme	ghrabhonos
Gmc.	*grabanam	grōba	grōbum	grabanaz
OHG.	graban²	gruob	gruobum	gigraban
MHG.	graben	gruop	gruoben	gegraben
NHG.	graben	grub	gruben	gegraben

CLASS VII

Goth.	haitan	haíhait	haíhaitum	haitans
OHG.	heizan	hiaz	hiazum	giheizan
MHG.	heizen	hiez	hiezen	geheizen
NHG.	heißen	hieß	hießen	geheißen

NOTES

1. Some verbs in Class I have a stem vowel $ē$: *lēh*, NHG. *lieh* (cf. Chapter 11, point (3)). Similarly some verbs in Class II have *ou* here: *boug*, NHG. *bog* (cf. Chapter 11, point (4)).

2. The forms of the singular of the present indicative are:

   for *ziohan: ziuhu, ziuhis, ziuhit*

for *helfan: hilfu, hilfis, hilfit*
for *neman: nimu, nimis, nimit*
for *geban: gibu, gibis, gibit*
for *graban: grabu, grebis, grebit*

3. *Kommen* belongs to Class IV and *sitzen* and *bitten* to Class V. How have these anomalous forms developed?

APPENDIX II

Specimen passages of German

Specimen passages illustrating German at various stages of its development and, for comparison, parallel passages in Gothic, Old English, and Dutch. All are translations of Luke I (26–31).

(For a wider selection of such parallel passages in German, see Fritz Tschirch, *1200 Jahre deutsche Sprache*, 1955.)

1. THE AUTHORISED VERSION OF THE BIBLE, 1611 (WITH MODERN SPELLING)

(26) And in the sixth month the angel Gabriel was sent from God unto a city of Galilee, named Nazareth, (27) To a virgin espoused to a man whose name was Joseph, of the house of David; and the virgin's name was Mary. (28) And the angel came in unto her, and said, Hail, thou that art highly favoured, the Lord is with thee: blessed art thou among women.

(29) And when she saw him, she was troubled at his saying, and cast in her mind what manner of salutation this should be. (30) And the angel said unto her, Fear not, Mary: for thou hast found favour with God. (31) And, behold, thou shalt conceive in thy womb, and bring forth a son, and shalt call his name Jesus.

HIGH GERMAN

2. TRANSLATION OF TATIAN'S GOSPEL HARMONY, FULDA, c. 830

(26) In themo sehsten manude gisentit uuard engil Gabriel fon gote in thie burg Galileę, thero namo ist Nazareth, (27) zi thiornun gimahaltero gommanne, themo namo uuas Joseph, fon huse Dauides, inti namo thero thiornun Maria. (28) Inti ingangenti thie engil zi iru quad: 'heil uuis thu gebono follu! truhtin mit thir, gisegenot sîs thû in uuîbun.'

(29) Tho siu thiu gisah, uuas gitruobit in sinemo uuorte inti thahta, uuelih uuari thaz uuolaqueti. (30) Quad iru ther engil: 'ni forhti thir, Maria, thu fundi huldi mit gote; (31) seno nu inphahis in reue inti gibiris sun inti ginemnis sinan namon Heilant.'

(Tatian lateinisch und deutsch, ed. Eduard Sievers, 2nd edn., 1892, p. 16)

150

Appendix II

3. THE FIRST GERMAN TRANSLATION OF THE WHOLE BIBLE, PUBLISHED BY JOHANN MENTEL AT STRASSBURG, 1466

(26) Wann in dem·vj·moned der engel gabriel wart gesant von gott in die stat galilee der name waz nazareth. (27) zů einer meide gemechelt eim man dez name was ioseph· von dem haus dauids: vnd der nam der meide waz maria. (28) Der engel gieng ein zů ir vnd sprach. Gegrússt seistu vol der genaden: der herr ist mit dir: du bist gesegent vnter den weiben.

(29) Do sy es gehort· sy wart betrúbt in seinem wort: vnd gedacht wie gethan dirr grůß wer. (30) Vnd der engel sprach zů ir. Nichten wǒlst dir fúrchten maria: wann du hast funden genad bey gott. (31) Sich du enpfechst im leip vnd gebirst einen sun: vnd du rúffest seinen namen ihesus.

(*Die erste deutsche Bibel*, ed. W. Kurrelmeyer, Vol. 1 (1904), pp. 197–98)

4. LUTHER'S TRANSLATION OF THE BIBLE

(a) *The first printed version of the New Testament* ('*September Testament*'), 1522

(26) Vnnd ym sechsten mond, ward der Engel Gabriel gesand von Gott, ynn eyne stadt ynn Gallilea, die heyst Nazareth, (27) zu eyner iungfrawen, die vertrawet war eynem man mit namen Joseph, von dem hauße Dauid, vnd der iungfrawen name heyst Maria, (28) vnd der Engel kam zu yhr hyneyn, vnd sprach, Gegrusset seystu holdselige, der herr ist mit dyr, du gebenedeyte vnter den weyben.

(29) Da sie aber yhn sahe, erschrack sie vber seyner rede, vnd gedacht, wilch eyn grus ist das. (30) Vnd der Engel sprach zu yhr, furcht dich nit Maria, du hast gnade funden bey Gott. (31) Sihe, du wirst schwanger werden ym leybe vnd eynen son geperen, des namen solltu Jhesus heyssen.

(b) *The last version published in Luther's life-time*, 1546

(26) VND im sechsten mond, ward der Engel Gabriel gesand von Gott, in eine stad in Galilea, die heisst Nazareth, (27) zu einer Jungfrawen, die vertrawet war einem Manne, mit namen Joseph, vom hause Dauid, und die iungfraw hies Maria. (28) Vnd der Engel kam zu jr hin ein, vnd sprach, Gegrůsset seistu holdselige, der HERR ist mit dir, du gebenedeiete vnter den Weibern.

(29) DA sie aber jn sahe, erschrack sie vber seiner rede, vnd gedachte, welch ein grus ist das? (30) Vnd der Engel sprach zu jr, Fúrchte dich nicht Maria, du hast gnade bey Gott funden. (31) Sihe, du wirst schwanger werden im Leibe, vnd einen Son geberen, des namen soltu Jhesus heissen.

(*Dr Martin Luthers Werke* [The Weimar edition]. *Die Deutsche Bibel*, vol. 6, 1929, pp. 210 and 211. The 1546 text has the following marginal notes: to verse 28: (Gebenedeiete) Das ist auff deudsch, Du Hochgelobte; to verse 30: (Gnade funden) Das ist, du hast einen gnedigen Gott.)

LOW GERMAN

5. LOW GERMAN TRANSLATION BASED ON LUTHER'S VERSION

(26) Unde im sôsten Mânte wart de Engel Gabriel gesent van Gade in eine Stadt in Galilea de hett Nazareth, (27) tho einer junckfrouwen de vortruwet was einem manne mit namen Joseph van dem huse David unde de junckfrouwe hete Maria. (28) Unde de Engel quam tho êr henin unde sprack: Gegrôtet systu hûldesalige de Here ys mith dy du gebenedyede manck den frouwen.

(29) Do se en ôuerst sach forschrack se auer syner rêde unde dachte: Wat ys dat vor ein groth. (30) Unde de Engel sprack tho êr: Furchte dy nicht Maria du heffst gnade by Gade ghefunden. (31) Sû du werst swanger werden im liue unde einen sône têlen des namen schaltu Jhesus heten.

(*Dat Nye Testament Martin Luthers*, Lübeck 1533, Folio XXX)

DUTCH

6. THE STATES GENERAL VERSION OF THE BIBLE

(26) Ende in de seste maent wiert de Engel Gabriel van Godt gesonden nae een stat in Galilea genaemt Nazareth, (27) Tot een Maeght die ondertrouwt was met eenen man, wiens name was Joseph, uyt den huyse Davids, ende de name der Maget was Maria. (28) Ende de Engel tot haer in gekomen zijnde, seyde, Weest gegroet ghy begenadighde, de Heere *is* met u, ghy *zijt* gezegent onder de vrouwen.

(29) Ende als zy *hem* sagh wiert sy seer ontroert over dit sijn woordt, ende overleyde hoedanige dese groetenisse mochte zijn. (30) Ende de Engel seyde tot haer, En vreest niet Maria, want ghy hebt genade by Godt gevonden. (31) Ende siet, ghy sult bevrucht worden, ende eenen sone baren, ende sult sijnen Name heeten JESUS.

(*Biblia, Dat is de gantsche heylige Schrifture* . . . t'Amsterdam. By Samuel Imbrecht en Gerbrant Schagen, 1662)

ENGLISH

7. AN OLD ENGLISH VERSION

(26) Soþlice on þam syxtan monðe wæs ásend Gabriel se engel fram drihtne on galilea ceastre. þære nama wæs nazaréth. (27) to beweddudre fæmnan ánum were. þæs nama wæs iosep. of dauides húse. and þære fæmnan nama wæs maria. (28) Ða cwæþ se engel ingangende. hál wes ðú mid gyfe gefylled: drihten mid þe; Ðu eart gebletsud on wifum.

(29) þa wearð heo on his spræce gedréfed. and þohte hwæt seo greting wære; (30) Ða cwæð se engel. ne ondræd þu ðe maría: Soðlice þu gyfe mid

gode gemettest; (31) Soðlice nu þu on innoðe ge-eacnast and sunu censt and his naman hælend genemnest.

(*The Gospel according to Saint Luke in Anglo-Saxon and Northumbrian versions*, ed. W. W. Skeat, 1874. Text from MS in Corpus Christi College, Cambridge)

GOTHIC

8. THE GOTHIC BIBLE OF BISHOP ULFILAS (DIED C. 383)

(26) þanuh þan in menoþ saihstin insandiþs was aggilus Gabriel fram guda in baurg Galeilaias sei haitada Nazaraiþ, (27) du magaþai in fragibtim abin, þizei namo Iosef, us garda Daweidis, jah namo þizos magaþais Mariam. (28) jah galeiþands inn sa aggilus du izai qaþ: fagino, anstai audahafta, frauja miþ þus; þiuþido þu in quinom.

(29) iþ si gasaiƕandei gaþlahsnoda bi innatgahtai is jah þahta sis ƕeleika wesi so goleins [þatei swa þiuþida izai]. (30) jah qaþ aggilus du izai: ni ogs þus, Mariam, bigast auk anst fram guda. (31) jah sai, ganimis in kilþein jah gabairis sunu jah haitais namo is Jesu.

(*Die gotische Bibel*, ed. W. Streitberg, Part I, 2nd edn., 1919, p. 87)

APPENDIX III

Bibliography

This bibliography contains only a very small selection of the many works on the history of the German language. It includes most of the standard handbooks and reference books, as well as a number of other more specialized monographs and introductory works. For the sake of convenience the books mentioned at the ends of chapters are included, except those following Chapters 1 and 4, which are of a more general kind. Many of the titles might have appeared under several different headings; they have been cited only once, at the point where they seemed most immediately relevant.

All the works listed contain further bibliography; readers should therefore have little difficulty in following up special interests. In particular Adolf Bach's *Geschichte der deutschen Sprache*, which frequently appears in new editions, contains full and up-to-date bibliographical references.

A. HISTORY OF THE GERMAN LANGUAGE (FROM INDO-EUROPEAN TO MODERN GERMAN)

1. *Handbooks* (*covering German literature and culture as well as language*)

Schwarz, Ernst, *Deutsche und germanische Philologie*, 1951
Stroh, Friedrich, *Handbuch der germanischen Philologie*, 1952
Stammler, Wolfgang (ed.), *Deutsche Philologie im Aufriß*, 3 vols. 2nd edn., 1956–60 (a composite work surveying the whole field of German and Germanic philology)

2. *General histories of German language*

Bach, Adolf, *Geschichte der deutschen Sprache*, 8th edn., 1965. Frequent new editions
Behaghel, Otto, *Die deutsche Sprache*, 13th edn., by Friedrich Maurer, 1958
Eggers, Hans, *Deutsche Sprachgeschichte*, 1963. 3 vols. have appeared
Hirt, Hermann, *Geschichte der deutschen Sprache*, 2nd. edn., 1925
Lockwood, William B., *An informal history of the German language, with chapters on Dutch and Afrikaans, Frisian and Yiddish*, 1965
Moser, Hugo, *Annalen der deutschen Sprache von den Anfängen bis zur Gegenwart*, 2nd edn., 1963 (Sammlung Metzler, No. 5)

154

Appendix III

Moser, Hugo, *Deutsche Sprachgeschichte, mit einer Einführung in die Fragen der Sprachbetrachtung*, 3rd edn., 1958

Priebsch, Robert C., and Collinson, William E., *The German Language*, 6th edn., 1966

Sperber, Hans, *Geschichte der deutschen Sprache*, 5th edn., by Peter von Polenz, 1966 (Sammlung Göschen, No. 915)

Tonnelat, Ernest, *Histoire de la langue allemande*, 4th edn., 1946

Tschirch, Fritz, *1200 Jahre deutsche Sprache. Die Entfaltung der deutschen Sprachgestalt in ausgewählten Stücken der Bibelübersetzung vom Ausgang des 8. Jahrhunderts bis in die Gegenwart*, 1955

Watermann, John T., *A history of the German language with special reference to the cultural and social forces that shaped the standard literary language*, 1966

3. Special periods

Krahe, Hans, *Sprache und Vorzeit*, 1954

Schrader, Otto, *Die Indogermanen*, 4th edn., by Hans Krahe, 1935

Porzig, Walter, *Die Gliederung des indogermanischen Sprachgebiets*, 1954

Lockwood, William B., *Indo-European Philology, Historical and Comparative*, 1969

Meillet, Antoine, *Caractères généraux des langues germaniques*, 7th edn., 1949

Maurer, Friedrich, *Nordgermanen und Alemannen: Studien zur germanischen und frühdeutschen Sprachgeschichte, Stammes- und Volkskunde*, 3rd edn., 1952

Schwarz, Ernst, *Goten, Nordgermanen, Angelsachsen: Studien zur Ausgliederung der germanischen Sprachen*, 1951

Schwarz, Ernst, *Germanische Stammeskunde*, 1956

Brooke, Kenneth, *An introduction to Early New High German*, 1955

Blackall, Eric A., *The emergence of German as a literary language 1700–1775*, 1958

Collinson, William E., *The German language today: its patterns and historical background*, 1953

Mackensen, Lutz, *Die deutsche Sprache unserer Zeit: Zur Sprachgeschichte des 20. Jahrhunderts*, 1956

B. VOCABULARY

1. General

Maurer, Friedrich, and Stroh, Friedrich (eds.), *Deutsche Wortgeschichte*, 3 vols., 2nd edn., 1959–60

Schirmer, Alfred, *Deutsche Wortkunde: eine kulturgeschichtliche Betrachtung des deutschen Wortschatzes*, 5th edn., by Walther Mitzka, 1965 (Sammlung Göschen, No. 929)

Mackensen, Lutz, *Deutsche Etymologie. Ein Leitfaden durch die Geschichte des deutschen Wortes*, 1962

Kretschmer, Paul, *Wortgeographie der hochdeutschen Umgangssprache*, 1918

2. Word-formation

Carr, Charles T., *Nominal compounds in Germanic*, 1939
Henzen, Walter, *Deutsche Wortbildung*, 3rd edn., 1965
Meid, Wolfgang, *Wortbildungslehre*, 1967 (Sammlung Göschen, No. 1218 a/b)

3. Loan words

Seiler, Friedrich, *Die Entwicklung der deutschen Kultur im Spiegel des deutschen Lehnworts*, 8 parts, 1913–24
Betz, Werner, *Der Einfluß des Lateinischen auf den althochdeutschen Sprachschatz. Der Abrogans*, 1936
Betz, Werner, *Deutsch und Lateinisch: die Lehnbildungen der althochdeutschen Benediktinerregel*, 1949
Ganz, Peter F., *Der Einfluß des Englischen auf den deutschen Wortschatz 1640–1815*, 1957
Palmer, Philip M., *The influence of English on the German vocabulary to 1800*, 1960

4. Semantics

Ullmann, Stephen, *Semantics: an introduction to the science of meaning*, 1962
Hatzfeld, Helmut A., *Leitfaden der vergleichenden Bedeutungslehre*, 2nd edn., 1928
Sperber, Hans, *Einführung in die Bedeutungslehre*, 3rd edn., 1965
Dornseiff, Franz, *Bezeichnungswandel unseres Wortschatzes*, 7th edn., 1966 (full title on p. 92)
Bahder, Karl von, *Zur Wortwahl in der frühneuhochdeutschen Schriftsprache*, 1925

C. GRAMMAR

1. Indo-European and Germanic

Brugmann, Karl, *Kurze vergleichende Grammatik der indogermanischen Sprachen*, 1904
Hirt, Hermann, *Indogermanische Grammatik*, 7 vols., 1921–37
Hudson-Williams, Thomas, *A short introduction to the study of comparative grammar (Indo-European)*, 1935
Krahe, Hans, *Indogermanische Sprachwissenschaft*, 2 vols., 3rd edn., 1958–9 (Sammlung Göschen, Nos. 59 and 64)

Hirt, Hermann, *Handbuch des Urgermanischen*, 3 vols., 1931–4
Krahe, Hans, *Germanische Sprachwissenschaft*, 2 vols., 3rd edn., 1956–7 (Sammlung Göschen, Nos. 238 and 780)
Prokosch, Eduard, *A comparative Germanic grammar*, 1939

Appendix III

2. Gothic, Old Norse, Old English

Braune, Wilhelm, *Gotische Grammatik*, 12th edn., by Karl Helm, 1947
Wright, Joseph, *A primer of the Gothic language with grammar, notes and glossary*, 2nd edn., 1899

Gordon, Eric V., *An introduction to Old Norse*, 2nd edn., by Arnold R. Taylor, 1957
Heusler, Andreas, *Altisländisches Elementarbuch*, 4th edn., 1950

Brook, George L., *An introduction to Old English*, 1955
Brunner, Karl, *Altenglische Grammatik nach der angelsächsischen Grammatik von Eduard Sievers*, 3rd edn., 1965

3. History of German sounds and forms

Kirk, Arthur, *An introduction to the historical study of New High German*, 1923
Horacek, Blanka, *Kleine historische Lautlehre des Deutschen*, 2nd edn., 1966
Karstien, Carl, *Historische deutsche Grammatik. I Geschichtliche Einleitung, Lautlehre*, 1939 (no more published)
Kienle, Richard von, *Historische Laut- und Formenlehre des Deutschen*, 1960
Meisen, Kurt, *Altdeutsche Grammatik*, 2 vols., 2nd edn., 1968 (Sammlung Metzler, Nos. 2 and 3)
Wright, Joseph, *Historical German Grammar*, Vol. 1: *Phonology, word-formation and accidence*, 1907 (no more published)

4. Old High German and Old Saxon

Armitage, Lionel, *An introduction to the study of Old High German*, 1911
Braune, Wilhelm, *Althochdeutsche Grammatik*, 9th edn., by Walther Mitzka, 1959
Ellis, Jeffrey, *An elementary Old High German grammar, descriptive and comparative*, 1953
Wright, Joseph, *An Old High German primer with grammar, notes and glossary*, 1906
Jolivet, Alfred and Mossé, Fernand, *Manuel de l'allemand du moyen âge des origines au XIVe siècle: grammaire, textes, glossaire*, 2nd edn., 1947

Holthausen, Ferdinand A. W., *Altsächsisches Elementarbuch*, 2nd edn., 1921

5. Middle High German and Middle Low German

Boor, Helmut de, and Wisniewski, Roswitha, *Mittelhochdeutsche Grammatik*, 1956 (Sammlung Göschen, No. 1108)
Eis, Gerhard, *Historische Laut- und Formenlehre des Mittelhochdeutschen*, 1950

A short history of the German language

Paul, Hermann, *Mittelhochdeutsche Grammatik*, 20th edn. by Hugo Moser and Ingeborg Schröbler, 1969

Weinhold, Karl, *Kleine mittelhochdeutsche Grammatik*, later edns., by Gustav Ehrismann, 11th edn., by Hugo Moser, 1955

Wright, Joseph, *Middle High German primer*, 5th edn., by Maurice O'C. Walshe, 1954

Lasch, Agate, *Mittelniederdeutsche Grammatik*, 1914

6. Early New High German and New High German

Moser, Virgil, *Frühneuhochdeutsche Grammatik* I, 1 *Orthographie, Betonung, Stammsilbenvokale;* III, 3 *Konsonanten*, 2. *Hälfte*, 1929, 1951

Paul, Hermann, *Deutsche Grammatik*, 5 vols., 1916–20

Stolte, Heinz, *Kurze deutsche Grammatik auf Grund der fünfbändigen deutschen Grammatik von Hermann Paul*, 3rd edn., 1962

7. Syntax

Behaghel, Otto, *Deutsche Syntax, eine geschichtliche Darstellung*, 4 vols., 1923–32

Dal, Ingerid, *Kurze deutsche Syntax*, 1952

Glinz, Hans, *Der deutsche Satz: Wortarten und Satzglieder wissenschaftlich gefaßt und dichterisch gedeutet*, 4th edn., 1965

Glinz, Hans, *Deutsche Syntax*, 2nd edn., 1967 (Sammlung Metzler, No. 43)

Lockwood, William B., *Historical German syntax*, 1968

8. Dialects

Keller, Rudolf E., *German dialects: phonology and morphology, with selected texts*, 1961

Mitzka, Walther, *Deutschen Mundarten*, 1943

Schwarz, Ernst, *Die deutschen Mundarten*, 1950

Henzen, Walther, *Schriftsprache und Mundarten: ein Überblick über ihr Verhältnis und ihre Zwischenstufen im Deutschen*, 2nd edn., 1954

D. DICTIONARIES AND LINGUISTIC ATLASES

Walde, Alois, and Pokorny, Julius, *Vergleichendes Wörterbuch der indogermanischen Sprachen*, 3 vols., 1928–32

Pokorny, Julius, *Indogermanisches etymologisches Wörterbuch*, Vol. 1, 1959, Vol. 2 (indices) in progress

Feist, Sigmund, *Vergleichendes Wörterbuch der gotischen Sprache*, 3rd edn., 1939

Cleasby, Richard, and Vigfússon, Gudbrand, *An Icelandic–English dictionary*, 1874

Bosworth-Toller, *An Anglo-Saxon dictionary based on the manuscript collections of the late Joseph Bosworth*. Edited by T. N. Toller, 1882–98. Supplement 1908–21

Appendix III

Schade, Oskar, *Altdeutsches Wörterbuch*, 2 vols., 2nd edn., 1872–82
Karg-Gasterstädt, Elisabeth, and Frings, Theodor, *Althochdeutsches Wörterbuch* 1952 – (in progress)

Holthausen, Ferdinand A. W., *Altsächsisches Wörterbuch*, 1954

Benecke, Georg F., Müller, Wilhelm, and Zarncke, Friedrich, *Mittelhochdeutsches Wörterbuch*, 3 vols. 1854–61,
Lexer, Matthias, *Mittelhochdeutsches Handwörterbuch*, 3 vols., 1872–8 (A supplement and index to Benecke–Müller–Zarncke.)
Lexer, Matthias, *Mittelhochdeutsches Taschenwörterbuch*, 30th edn., 1961 (Originally an abridgement of the *Handwörterbuch*, but frequently revised and expanded. The most convenient dictionary for general purposes.)
Lübben, August, and Walther, Christoph, *Mittelniederdeutsches Handwörterbuch*, 1888
Lasch, Agate, Borchling, Conrad, and Cordes, Gerhard, *Mittelniederdeutsches Handwörterbuch*, 1919 – (in progress)

Götze, Alfred, *Frühneuhochdeutsches Glossar*, 6th edn., 1960
Grimm, Jakob, and Grimm, Wilhelm, *Deutsches Wörterbuch*, 32 vols., 1854–1960 (A second edition began to appear in 1965.)
Götze, Alfred, and Mitzka, Walther, *Trübners Deutsches Wörterbuch*, 8 vols., 1939–57
Paul, Hermann, *Deutsches Wörterbuch*, 5th edn., by Werner Betz, 1957–66
Spalding, Keith, and Brooke, Kenneth, *An historical dictionary of German figurative usage*, 1959(1952) – (in progress)

Kluge, Friedrich, *Etymologisches Wörterbuch der deutschen Sprache*, 18th edn., by Walther Mitzka, 1960
Walshe, Maurice O'C., *A concise German etymological dictionary. With a supplement on the etymology of some Middle High German words extinct in modern German*, by Marianne Winder, 1951
Der große Duden: Etymologie. Herkunftswörterbuch der deutschen Sprache, 1963

Wrede, Ferdinand, *Deutscher Sprachatlas*, continued by Walther Mitzka and Bernhard Martin, 1927–56
Mitzka, Walther, and Schmitt, Ludwig E., *Deutscher Wortatlas*, 1951 – (in progress)

Index

Index

This index contains only the main references to names and topics; many minor or incidental references have been omitted. Entries under names of languages or dialects often contain reference to the speakers and to the regions or countries where they are or were spoken.

163

Index

Index

Gothic, Goths, 15, 20, 21, 23, 24, 27, 73, 129, 135
Göttingen, 35, 47
Gottsched, Johann Christoph, 48, 49
grammatical change, *see* Verner's Law
Greek, 11, 14, 26, 27, 28, 135; loan-words from 73–4, 92
Grimm, Jakob, 29, 42, 50, 98, 117, 129
Grimm, Wilhelm, 50, 117
Gutenberg, Johann, 29

Halle, 47
Hansa, 36, 37
Harsdörffer, Georg Philipp, 49
Heinrich von Veldeke, 34
Herder, Johann Gottfried, 3, 50, 80
Herminones, 20, 24
Hildebrandslied, 32
Hindi, 13
Hittite, 11, 15
humanism, 39, 42, 46, 72, 78
Hungarian, loan-words from, 77

Icelandic, Iceland, 20, 23
Illyrian, 13, 15, 20, 71
incapsulation, 136
Indian languages, 11, 12, 13, 15
indirect speech, 135, 137, 142–3
Indo-European, 4, 5, 9 ff., 17, 56, 58, 60, 118; accent, 10; conjugations, 10, 128, 142; consonants, 9; declensions, 10, 119, 120, 123; development of inflexional system, 10; languages developed from, 13 ff.; loan-words in, 15, 71; original home of, 11–13; syntax, 135; vocabulary, 11, 12, 56, 57; vowels, 9
infinitive: in IE., 10, 128; inflected, in German, 132, 141, 142; position of, 137; accusative and infinitive, 136
Ingaevones ('Ingwäonen'), 20, 24
Iranian languages, 13, 15
Ireland, 28
Istaevones, 20, 24
Italian, Italy, 14, 20, 45; loan-words from, 77–8
Italic languages, 14, 15, 26

Japan, loan-words from, 79
Julius Caesar, 17

Langobardic (Lombardic), 20, 23, 112
language: colloquial, 32; methods of

study of, 4 ff.; nature of, 1 ff.; origins of, 3 f.
Latin, 14, 18, 26, 27, 28, 32, 33, 35, 46, 47, 48, 69, 91, 92, 136; loan-words from 72–3, 74, 78; loan translations from, 75
Lausitz, 36, 37
Lech, river, 22
Leibniz, Gottfried Wilhelm, 49
Leipzig, 38, 44, 47, 49
Lettish, Latvia, 14, 45
lingua romana, 133
literary languages, 32, 33; MHG., 34, 35, 104; Netherlandish (Dutch and Flemish), 36; NHG., 40, 41, 42, 43, 44, 46, 47, 48, 49, 50, 51, 104; regional, in fourteenth to sixteenth centuries, 36, 37, 38, 39
literature: courtly, 34, 35, 76; German, 39; OHG., 32, 33, 104; MHG., 33; vernacular, 46
Lithuanian, Lithuania, 14, 45
loan translation, 71, 75, 77, 80, 91, 92
loan-words, 69, 70, 85, 89, 91, 100; excessive use of, 48, 80–1; and foreign words, 70; from dialects, 78; from professional and group languages, 79; *see also names of individual languages and countries*
Logau, Friedrich von, 49
long words, 67
Lorraine, 45
Luther, Martin, 40, 41, 42, 43, 46, 47, 49, 80; Bible, 42, 43; New Testament, 41; vocabulary of, 42
Lycian, 15
Lydian, 15

Magdeburg, 37
Main, river, 20, 21, 37
Mainz, 21, 29, 39
Malberg glosses, 27
Manx, 14
meaning, change of (semantic change), 82 ff.; abstract to concrete, 85, concrete to abstract, 85, extension, 83, improvement, 84, restriction, 83, worsening, 84
Meissen, 36, 37, 38
metaphor, 87
metonymy, 87
migrations (*Völkerwanderung*), 18
monasteries, 32, 73, 74

Index

Silesian, Silesia, 14, 36, 37, 43, 44
Sinhalese, 13
Slavonic languages, 11, 14, 15
Slovak, Slovakia, 14, 45
Slovene, 14
Sorb, 14
Sound-Shift: First (Germanic), 18, 99 ff.; Second (High German), 23, 72, 112 f.
Spanish, 14; loan-words from, 79
spelling: reforms in, 51; uniformity in, 50
Speyer, 21
Sprachgesellschaften, 48–9, 80
standard languages, *see* literary languages
St Gallen, 32
subjunctive, 128, 129, 132; uses of, 51, 142, 143
substratum theory, 17 f., 100
suffixes, 118, 128, 129; borrowed from French, 76; Latin, 74; forming nouns, 65, adjectives, 65, 66, verbs, 66
Sumerian, 4, 26
Swabian, Swabia, 22, 35, 39
Swedish, Swedes, 20, 23
Switzerland, 22, 43, 51
syllable: unaccented, 34, 108 f., 121
synthetic languages, 118

Tacitus, 17, 20
tenses: IE., 10, 128; Gmc., 128; compound, 133; future, 133; perfect, 133; pluperfect, 133; sequence of, 135, 143
Tepl, Johann von, 39
Thomasius, Christian, 47, 49
Thracian, 15
Thuringian, Thuringia, 21, 23, 37, 39
Tirol, South, 45
Tocharian, 15
Trier (Trèves), 21, 28
Turkish, loan-words from, 79
type (in printing); Antiqua, 29; Fraktur, 29; roman, 29

Ulfilas, bishop, 21, 27–8, 135
Umbrian, 14

umlaut (modification of vowels), 106, 122; primary, 106; secondary, 107 f.
universities, 46, 50; technical vocabulary of, 69
Urdu, 13

Vandals, 20
Vedic, 13
Venetic, 15
verbs: IE., 10, 128, 142; Gmc., 31, 128, 129, 142; German, 129 ff.; auxiliary, 133, 134; compound, 62; continuous forms, 141; derivative, 66; inflexional endings, 129, 131, 132, 142; modal auxiliary, 141, 142; position of, 136, 137; preterito-present, 132; strong, 10, 99, 129, 130, 131; weak, 10, 18, 66, 129, 131
Verner's Law, 102, 114
Vienna, 39
Vikings, 20
Vistula, river, 20
vocabulary, Chs. 7, 8, 9; IE., 11, 12, 56, 57; Luther's, 42; of mystics, 34, 76–7; of science and technology, 92
voice, in verbs: IE., 10, 128; Gmc., 128; passive, 134
vowels: IE., 9; Gmc., 95 ff.; OHG., 105 ff.; MHG., 108 f.; NHG., 109 ff.

Weimar, 48
Welsh, 14
Werra, river, 21
Weser, river, 20
Wittenberg, 43, 44
Wolff, Christian, 49
word-fields, 86
Worms, 21
Würzburg, 21, 37

Yiddish, 46

Zesen, Philipp von, 49
Ziegler, Niclas, 39
Zips, 45
Zürich, 43
Zuyder Zee, 21
Zwingli, Ulrich, 43

167